Forging a
REALWORLD
FAITH

Forging a R*EAL* W*ORLD* F*AITH*

Gordon MacDonald

OLIVER
NELSON

A Division of Thomas Nelson Publishers
Nashville

Published in Nashville, Tennessee, by Oliver-Nelson Books, a division of Thomas Nelson, Inc., Publishers, and distributed in Canada by Lawson Falle, Ltd., Cambridge, Ontario.

Unless otherwise noted, Scripture quotations are taken from the HOLY BIBLE: NEW INTERNATIONAL VERSION. Copyright © 1973, 1978, 1984 by the International Bible Society. Used by permission of Zondervan Bible Publishers.

Scripture quotations noted TEV are from the *Good News Bible*. Old Testament: Copyright © American Bible Society 1976; New Testament: Copyright © American Bible Society 1966, 1971, 1976. Used by permission.

Scripture quotations noted TLB are taken from *The Living Bible,* copyright 1971 by Tyndale House Publishers, Wheaton, IL. Used by permission.

Scripture quotations noted NKJV are from THE NEW KING JAMES VERSION. Copyright © 1979, 1980, 1982, Thomas Nelson, Inc., Publishers.

Printed in the United States of America.

Library of Congress Cataloging-in-Publication Data

MacDonald, Gordon.
    Forging a real world faith / Gordon MacDonald.
      p. cm.
    ISBN 0-8407-9016-3
    1. Christian life—1960– 2. MacDonald, Gordon. I. Title.
BV4501.2.M2265 1989   89–38709
248.4—dc20   CIP

1 2 3 4 5 6 — 94 93 92 91 90 89

Contents

Acknowledging

A remarkable wife, Gail, who works with me through every word of a manuscript. Each book with the MacDonald name on it is always a product of teamwork.

A special friend, Victor Oliver, my publisher now of six books. Encourager, fellow Christ-follower.

A team of quality people: the men and women at Thomas Nelson who edit my writing, arrange for its distribution in many different languages, and see to it that I feel good about what I am doing.

A congregation of "alive" people at Trinity Baptist Church in New York City who are following Jesus through the "streets" of New York and giving Gail and me the chance to serve them with pastoral care.

Introduction

In the past ten years of my life I've passed through three discernible seasons of the spirit. By seasons, I mean times of enhanced personal need, newly acquired insight, and new resolutions about what was really important to me. It would not have occurred to me that this was so obvious except that my wife, Gail, pointed it out to me when she finished reading a first draft of this book.

"The flow of the book conforms to the things you've been going through and then writing about," she observed. And after I'd pondered what she had said, I realized Gail was correct.

The first season came when I experienced a personal renaissance as I became aware of how much I needed to learn about the person of God and what it meant to worship Him. That opened the door to the kind of thinking I reflected in the writing of a book called *Ordering Your Private World*.

Then in another period of life I was forced through personal failure to take a long, hard look deep within myself. The look was not entirely pleasant. I came to understand how vulnerable all of us are to fatigue, confusion of spirit, distortion of values, and the numbness of disillusionment. But most important, I discovered the reality of inner evil—not in others, but in myself. In the wake of a very dark moment, I wrote *Renewing Your Spiritual Passion* and, a couple of years later, *Rebuilding Your Broken World*.

During this dark season the perspective was not all gloomy. I learned what so many others have learned who have drunk freely at the wellspring of grace: God is kind and restorative when men and women take their sins seriously and approach Him in brokenness. My experience was that He responds not only with forgiveness but also with insights and opportunities that one could hardly have imagined. One meets a whole new population of people: the hurting, the broken, the bewildered, the folks who are scared to expose their failures and their wounds because they've heard from some that there is no way back. As long as my world had appeared to be impervious to struggle or failure, I rarely met those men and women. But once some of them knew that I was conversant with humiliation and remorse, an amazing thing happened; I learned about the underside of the community of Christian faith.

And now there's a third season of the spirit beginning to emerge in my personal world. It connects with a decision Gail and I made to move to New York City and join a special group of people who asked if we would be a part of their congregational life.

When they first invited us to come to New York, we quickly told them, no thanks. People entering their fifties, we assumed, had no business entering an urban culture that foreign to previous life experience. Besides, we thought to ourselves, you know what everyone thinks of New York City.

But those were thoughts that came to us *before* we came to understand what God thinks of New York City. Guess what: He loves the place and its people! And not enough of us know that.

New York City fully aroused within me something that had been brewing for many years: the renewed challenge of insisting that my life of following Christ be absolutely nose to nose with what is going on in the "streets" where people live and work. Suddenly, I found myself going off to the office every day with a reenergized vision of discovering how Jesus would engage people and situations were this the time and place of His incarnation.

When I saw the homeless man sleeping over the subway grate, when I heard the ceaseless sirens of the police ambulance, when I read the news of the latest drug bust, when I smelled the strong odor of urine in the subway station, and when I felt the instant anger arise within me because someone ripped me off for forty dollars, I knew that I was in a world I had never seen or taken seriously before. If I were to survive and make some small contribution in it, I'd have to know what it means to follow Jesus into it.

And when I saw a well-known celebrity alight from a stretch limo, when I heard the thunderous roar of the traders on the stock market floor demanding attention for their bid, when I read the society column's description of the latest yacht party on the East River, when I smelled the aroma of dinners in restaurants whose prices one can only guess at, and when I felt the instant sense of awe arise within me in response to the magnificent architecture of the new skyscrapers, I also knew that I was in a world I had never seen or taken seriously before. If I were to survive and make some small contribution among *these* people and in *these places,* I'd have to know what it meant to follow Jesus into this part of the city also.

And that was the origin for this third season of the spirit. A renaissance, if you please: a new set of questions about how one follows Christ into such a complex, treacherous, and beautiful place. How does one who cares the slightest bit about faith in God live in a place like this? Answer that question, and you are liable to understand how one can live through faith in any other part of the world. For here—in this city—there is the best of the best and the worst of the worst.

Ever since we moved to New York City, I have enjoyed a weekly breakfast with a physician who has become a good friend. We always eat at the Silver Star Cafe on Second Avenue; we sit at the same table; and we order the same things: decaffeinated coffee, a melon, and an order of whole wheat toast. And then we talk.

We usually talk about our work: mine as a pastor and an author; his as an orthopedic surgeon who helps broken hips and other assorted troubled bones heal back into working order. We also talk about what we're reading and learning, how we're doing in our family lives, where God is in our spiritual journeys, and whether or not each of us is getting too tired or overworked. It's a good friendship, and it provides a point of accountability for both of us as men who have a desire to continue growing.

One day my friend said to me (and I liberally paraphrase his words), "I try to go to the hospital every morning with the high-minded intention of serving every person I meet—the patients, the hospital personnel, and my colleagues. But I discover that by noontime I can barely remember the ideals I began the day with. Now it's a fight just to survive for the rest of the day. New York can be a disabling place."

Just this morning my friend spoke again of his medical world, and I heard him say something like this: "The majority of people I work with would never consider any spiritual dimension to a decision in the hospital's life. In fact, if anyone were to suggest that prayer, biblical study, or any sort of Christian value was of use in the solving of our problems, he would probably be laughed out of the room. Christ simply isn't an option! What is an option is what will advance medical science, increase the revenue of the hospital and physicians' salaries, win grant money, and enhance professional prestige."

I realized that I was hearing similar comments from the business executives I met at lunch, the diplomats I met at the United Nations, and the artists I met over on Broadway. So it has been out of these observations that I have entered into this third season of the spirit: a renewed awareness of a world that is broken and beautiful at the same time and the accompanying questions of how a person committed to Jesus lives in the midst of it.

One day someone said to me of New York City, "This is certainly the real world." And I was about to agree when a thought came: *No, there is more to the real world than just a city.* And I began to fool with terms.

Real world: a paradox in words, for in the strictest sense the word *world* describes our global place, its peoples, and its natural systems. It's a limited place, and reality is not limited. To a person who believes the Bible, reality expands far beyond the world, far beyond the limits of the universe, to a place called Heaven whose boundaries and dimensions boggle the mind. But that's also reality.

So I did what poets often do. I created my own word—*real-world*—and I assigned three dimensions of reality to it. First is the place the Bible calls Heaven where the Everlasting God, Creator of everything, dwells. The second dimension is the inner space of the human being with all its darkness and its potential beauty. And the third dimension is the streets upon which we live out our lives as we work, play, love, and struggle.

As the book will reveal, I developed a second special word: *Christ-follower.* I did this—as I'll also explain—because I have been increasingly dissatisfied with the word *Christian.* The two words—*Christian* and *Christ-follower*—really mean the same thing, but the word *Christian* has lost its punch. It hardly means a thing any longer, and usually when it is employed among those who consider themselves non-Christians, it is used pejoratively. On the other hand, *Christ-following* is a dynamic term. It drips with action, direction, challenge. So I've taken the risk of using it wherever I would formerly have used the word *Christian.*

And then I've used the word *forging* to suggest a process of faith development. I hope to put forth the idea that every Christ-follower must take seriously the management of his or her faith. Of course, this is done under the supervision of God's Holy Spirit. It would be presumptuous to think otherwise.

But I see faith as the process of Christ-following through the real world, and I see it as a vigorous, almost violent, process, carried on every day with accompanying bumps and scrapes. I see it as something that calls for us to take risks and not to be afraid of making errors of judgment.

So a real-world faith is one in which a person follows Jesus into all three dimensions. And that is exactly what I have been trying to do over these past years, and they have formed the seasons of my spirit: from the Heavenlies to the inner parts to the streets, always—thankfully—in the company of Jesus, a most gentle yet very demanding guide.

It will not take much insight for anyone to see that *Forging a Real-World Faith* is not a book for serious theologians. Put this volume in their hands, and they will raise a thousand challenging questions, and that's OK. No, I write for the men and women who have to pound out a living on those streets, who feel beaten up on a daily basis not by muggers coming out of alleys but by muggers who will do anything to take away confidence and self-respect in the job or on the commuter trip or in the marketplace. I want to wrestle with the "old, old story" with some new words and some adventurous ideas.

Where I've been less than complete in my thinking, or when I haven't raised the best of the possible questions, forgive me. I just want to maintain the momentum of the questions in these three seasons of the spirit. So join me at the anvil and do some pounding yourself. A real-world faith starts emerging from the fire when one or more people turn to Jesus and say, "I will follow You. Where do we start?" And I hear Him say to us, "There are three places I'd like to visit with you."

GORDON MACDONALD,
New York City
Canterbury, New Hampshire

FORGING A REAL-WORLD FAITH

is

following Christ to meet God
in the real world of the Heavenlies

. . . .

following Christ to master self
in the real world of the inner being

. . . .

following Christ to make history
in the real world of the streets

CHAPTER ONE

Swing Your
Own Hammer!

A Thought for You, Smithy
Get your fire started, Smithy, and make it hot.
You have a faith to hammer into shape today. Its
design must please the One who called you to this
significant task.

I have visited a blacksmith's shop only once. It looked exactly like the ones I'd seen previously in western films. A dumpy old shack with an open front, bits and pieces of metal stacked or shelved everywhere, and a variety of soot-covered farm implements and tools that looked as if they had been waiting patiently for years to be repaired. There seemed a disorder to everything, kind of a picture of my study during a writing project.

The smithy I came to watch was a robust, sweaty man dressed in coveralls who worked in intense heat near an open fire called a *forge*. In his hand was an enormous hammer, the most frequently used tool in the process of *forging*. His "desk" was a black iron anvil, and upon it he rested a thick, superheated metal rod. I watched as he repeatedly struck the almost-molten piece with his hammer, creating a spectacular shower of sparks.

At first I had the impression that the man was simply swinging his hammer wildly like a child releasing excess energy or rage. But it soon became clear that there was a purpose to every strike, for as it slowly yielded to the well-aimed blows, the rod was shaped to become a replacement for a part in a piece of farm machinery that lay nearby.

The forging process took a while because the contour of the part was unusual. Whenever the cooling metal became unyielding to the

15

blows of his hammer, the smithy returned it to the fire, pumped a set of bellows with his foot, and caused the flame to become all the more furious. The metal had no chance; it was only a matter of time until the man with the hammer had his way with it.

The brilliance of the hot metal in the fire, the loud clang of the hammer on the anvil, and the feel of the heat in that shop have remained in my bank of memories for years. And I have often drawn upon that experience to form a metaphor of what it might mean to forge a faith capable of functioning in *every* sphere of my life.

I am aware that the English verb to *forge*, can be used in at least two different ways. One can forge (or falsify) another's signature on a check and go to prison for it. Or one can, like a smithy, forge (or develop) a unique tool for a special project and be paid handsomely for it.

Using the first definition, I suppose that one could forge an appearance of some kind of faith using correct words, creeds, and ceremonial actions and manage to impress a lot of people before time and analysis proved the counterfeit nature of it all.

On the other hand, forging a faith might also mean managing a belief-process which gradually (sometimes slowly; sometimes swiftly) fans out through one's life and all its extensions (who I am, what I do, and what I own) to produce a person after the creative designs of the Heavenly Maker.

There are many kinds of faith, of course. We all have to have a kind of faith in certain people, for example, or in natural laws, or in a national currency. Life could become rather bleak if we refused to do this and locked ourselves into a suspicion of everything. Stock markets crash, companies go bellyup (as they say), and politicians get the sack when the public loses faith in them. In these situations we are talking about a general form of faith that amounts to confidence and trust.

But I intend to talk about something far more specific; start by calling it biblical faith. This is a kind of life-oriented confidence that begins when a person chooses, as the New Testament writer puts it, to believe that God exists and that humanity is accountable to Him (see Heb. 11:6).

Both Testaments offer multiple examples of this kind of faith. In the Older Testament men and women practice biblical faith when they affirm the trustworthiness and loving-kindness of the God of Abraham, Isaac, and Jacob and prove their declarations through unquestioning obedience to the things He calls upon them to do.

In the New Testament the same kind of faith appears when men and women avow the credibility of Jesus (whom I affirm as the Son of God) and set out to follow Him. So the concept of faith from both ends of the Bible is the same: trustworthiness and credibility—to obey and to follow—amount to the same thing and produce similar results.

Biblical faith always begins with a choice; it enlarges in a dynamic sense into all dimensions of life; and finally, it culminates in a total refining of all God meant us to be when He willed us into being. Because this biblical faith was best taught and modeled by Jesus, I also like to call it *Christ-following faith*.

Earlier I said that this biblical or Christ-following faith must be extended to "every sphere of my life." That's important to add because I have discovered, much to my consternation, that there have been occasions when I entered or was pushed into a new sphere of reality—a sudden choice, an unprecedented challenge, an unexpected crisis—and my faith was not enlarged enough. This is not God's fault; it is quite likely to be my own.

Of course I am not unique in this problem. One of my favorite Bible stories illustrates the matter quite nicely at the expense of Jesus' disciples. One evening as they crossed the Lake of Galilee with Jesus resting in one of their boats, a ferocious storm blew up. The bravado of these experienced lake-sailors disintegrated as boats began to swamp, and they rushed to the sleeping Jesus, demanding, "Don't you care if we drown?" Jesus awoke, calmed the storm, and made an interesting comment to the astonished men, "Do you still have no faith?" (Mark 4:35–41).

What could He have meant by His remark? Didn't they have at least a bit of faith when they chose to follow Him in the first place? Of course. But He was speaking of that dynamic element of faith, the part that is supposed to enlarge to fit each circumstance. And their faith had clearly not yet expanded to meet storm specifications.

What could Jesus have been expecting of His men? Perhaps that they would have taken note of His sleeping posture and assumed that they also were safe: that it was smart to simply point the boat into the wind and ride out the tempest. That would have been dynamic faith.

I have also discovered spheres where the faith I had didn't seem to fit very well, didn't provide the direction and principle I needed, and so I unconsciously assumed that faith had no relevance there. But most of us know that such faith, which fails to perform universally in our lives, is poor and inadequate indeed.

It has been common to speak critically of the person who practices a version of Christ-following faith on weekends but leaves it in the parking lot on Monday morning only to pick it up again on Friday evening. This is usually said to poke at the person who lives what is called a double life. But that may be too simple a judgment. Perhaps some leave their faith in the parking lot not because they want to, but because the faith they have simply has not been enlarged and shaped to fit the conditions of weekday realities. This may not be hypocrisy; it may simply be a failure to understand that the faith Jesus taught and to which He called people was designed to operate most effectively on the streets and not in the church.

The smithy in farm country hammers and shapes his hot metal to produce a part that will stand up under every sort of duress that field life presents. The person who ponders the forging of a faith thinks (or should think) similarly:

How can I develop a faith that will function every day in the routines and the unexpected situations and that will not bend or snap under any circumstance?

This salient question naturally tempts me back toward the task of definition. What is this faith that must be forged? I honestly shrink before the question because I know that scholars have been working on the matter for many centuries, and I do not include myself in their league. I have this suspicion that faith is more easily observed than defined; that you know it when you see it. So I'd rather describe it than define it.

After they have exhausted their vocabularies and thought-forms, theologians will probably find it difficult to improve upon a profound comment found in the New Testament: "To have faith is to be sure of the things we hope for, to be certain of the things we cannot see" (Heb. 11:1 TEV).

This lively statement speaks of faith not as an abstract term but as an action of one's inner being: *to be sure, to be certain*. It really doesn't tell you what faith is; it simply tells you what happens when you have it. The writer refers to a working awareness of realities that transcend the limits of what a person can see, hear, taste, touch, or smell.

The subsequent paragraphs go on to describe faith by telling the stories of a dozen or more men and women who accomplished some amazing things that were pleasures to God. They won battles, presided over miracles, endured incredible hardships, and even overcame death itself. In this section of the Bible the definition of faith flies on the wings of stories not of precise definitions.

Boil all of the stories down, and you come to an awareness that the central characters possessed three things (and here you have a simple outline of this entire book):

1. They possessed a certainty about how to meet and commune with their God.

2. They gained a remarkable degree of self-control as they came to understand the importance of the power of God filling their interior lives.

3. They came to see that all of us make a bit of history and that it was vital to make that history in accord with the purposes of God.

To borrow a phrase: in God they trusted, so they had little or no fear about the sort of things that might intimidate other people. When they looked within themselves, they seemed to own a clear inventory of their weaknesses and their strengths and how those should be managed to advantage. And what about the history they were making? They seemed to be guided by a dream or a mission that absorbed them and made sense out of life's little and large details.

Having this remarkable threefold perspective, they became models for us all, the Bible says, and they are portrayed as a "cloud of witnesses." I prefer to see them like a crowd of retired athletes sitting in the stadium cheering on their successors: those whose faith is also reflected in that threefold perspective. I am both fascinated and not a little anxious over the fact that they are sitting in that grandstand watching me. Come share my fascination and anxiety; they watch you also. Do they have much to cheer about as we compete?

How does this faith develop? And in the simplest terms, what does it look like?

A friend of mine owns a large sailboat. He invites me to join him one evening for a short voyage on the Long Island Sound. When we arrive at the dock, he asks me to wait while he goes aboard and prepares a few things. Then when he is ready, he waves for me to join him. Unsure of myself, I climb onto the boat feeling quite awkward and making self-deprecating jokes about my lack of familiarity with a sailor's world.

Knowing that my sailing experience is limited, he offers some basic instruction when I've joined him. "I want to put your mind at ease so that you can have a great time when we get out on the water. Re-

member two things. First, this boat cannot tip over no matter what
your senses tell you, and second, it cannot sink."

It can't tip over, he says, because of something to do with the
relationship between the area of the sail and the size of the keel under
the boat. And it can't sink because of the construction of the hull. I
don't understand all of this subsequent explanation, and it's not really
important to me. But the initial assertions—no tipping over; no
sinking—and the fact that my friend has made them are important.
Understanding the facts about sail, keel, and construction is not as
essential to me as accepting the word of the owner of the boat.

I trust my friend's thorough knowledge of his boat and the sea, and
I am content to enjoy myself as a result. That's faith: both my choice
to rely on his judgment *and* my choice to have a good time. So later
when the wind begins to blow rather vigorously and the boat leans so
far over that the gunwale is almost in the water, and every bone in my
body tells me we're about to capsize, I master my natural instinct to
panic because my friend tells me that the boat can't tip over. And then
when a wave crashes over the bow and bathes me and the deck with
water, I refuse to worry because my friend also assures me that the
boat can't sink. That's faith too.

Soon, having trusted him and mastered my feelings, I am relaxed,
enjoying this challenging experience. He even "orders" me to take
the wheel while he works with the jib up front. I become more and
more exhilarated by the relationship of the wind and sail and how I can
do my part to cause the boat to plunge ahead toward our destination.
In effect, I am helping to make a little of the history aboard the sailing
vessel. Perhaps my name will even be entered upon the log as having
been at the helm under orders from the owner. All of that is faith also.

So what is faith in this story? It begins when I accept the owner's
invitation to come aboard. It grows as I take his word about realities
I'm not yet personally experienced enough to perceive. And it ma-
tures as I involve myself with the whole process and even participate
in making the voyage happen.

When the scholars get started, the word *faith* takes on a score of
meanings constructed in carefully chosen words. It would be beneath
them to fool with stories about sailboats. Studying their definitions I
learn that *faith* is an expandable word. At one moment, it can reflect a
specific act, or at another moment, it can describe one's entire view of
how life is to be lived and to whom one might be accountable for that
mode of living.

Now let me introduce the other key word for use in this book; it's a modifier: *real-world*. It's one of those compound terms we begin to use in English when the original word loses its ability to grab our imaginations. We associate the *real world* with everything in reality that lies beyond the perimeter of what we perceive to be safety for ourselves. For example, if my home is a pleasant place with loving relationships, I am liable to say in the morning, "It's time to leave and go out into the real world where they compete and sometimes beat you up." If my church is a pleasing experience, I am liable to say to my pastor, "What you're telling me works well here in this building, but out there in the real world . . ." It's a term guaranteed to deflate any preacher whom you would like to momentarily neutralize.

Having a real-world faith, then, means trusting God or following Christ outside the harbor where things get rough. Or—may I please repeat myself, switching metaphors, for the sake of emphasis—*to forge a real-world faith is to hammer out a functioning certainty about meeting and getting to know God; it is to shape a capacity to understand and master my inner self; and it is, finally, to bring into being a conviction about how the history I make is congruent with the purposes of the Lord*. Beyond that, forging a real-world faith implies that these three things are possible in every circumstance.

The English words *faith* and *believe* have always been treated as virtually synonymous when they are related to the content of the Bible. And Christians (to whom I will now begin to refer as Christ-followers) are those who have heard the Bible to say that one's relationship to God, to oneself, and to one's times is built upon confidence in Jesus. They affirm that confidence and live in accord with it.

Leaving the smithy's shop once again and heading back to the harbor, I find it helpful to imagine that Jesus is the owner of the boat upon which I might make my life's voyage. He invites me aboard, and I show a specific act of faith when I accept His invitation. When I get aboard, He begins to infuse me with confidence. He affirms that the boat isn't going to tip over and won't sink, and I conclude that He's believable. He determines where the boat is to go, and I'm given the chance to do things like steer it. As I do all this—and do it with reasonable calmness of spirit—I demonstrate in act and attitude the basics of real-world faith.

When Christ-followers talk about this real-world faith theologically, they begin by talking about *saving faith,* that initial choice a person makes to turn from other "gods" and to embrace Christ, the Mediator between God and humanity.

In ancient days the "gods" from whom people turned were usually deities of one type or another. You built altars to them, made sacrifices that might even include a child or two, and kept yourself in a perpetual state of fear about their unreliable whims. No fun "sailing" with those gods.

In modern times, in developed places, gods may not be old-fashioned deities; rather, they may be compelling goals, desires, or spiritualist perspectives. Career-oriented success and its rewards or a form of psychological well-being can easily become a god to many. A contemporary "god" can actually be a sought-after lifestyle of hedonistic pleasure or the obvious compulsion to wealth that makes some people do strange and risky things. Most of us are aware that these gods aren't a lot more reliable than the ancient ones.

Whether it be the gods of ancient times or the new ones (and some may argue that there is little difference), gods are all-consuming, and like it or not, we all serve one of them. Or we choose to follow Christ.

If He is the One we have chosen to follow, there is the lifelong process of following. Not a simple matter! One would like to know right from the beginning where Christ is going to lead. The specifics are often kept a mystery. (That's probably a mercy since most of us couldn't handle the information.) But I would like to suggest that we can be certain about the directions we will be going.

Meeting God

To follow Christ is *to walk with Him* first into the presence of His Father. If that is so, we had better know how to act in the divine presence *now* (in this present life) and *then* (in the life everlasting). Ultimately, we will be there a long, long time. Finding out how to function there when we meet Him is part of forging a real-world faith.

Mastering Self

To follow Christ is *to walk with Him* through an extensive exploration of our inner selves. If that is so, we had better know how to act when He helps us uncover our defects and discover our potentials. Knowing what to do at both times is part of forging a real-world faith.

Making "History"

To follow Christ is *to walk with Him* through our public worlds, the safe and the unsafe parts as we make our own private histories and respond to the mission He has fashioned for us. If that is so, we had better know where He wishes to lead and what He has called us to achieve. Doing that is part of forging a real-world faith.

Let me be candid at the very beginning: I have dared to tackle this subject because I have the conviction that the faith many of us have forged simply will not engage the realities of this century-changing time of our history.

I did not say this of the faith Christ imparted to us. Rather, I am saying it of the faith we think we have heard and mixed liberally with our own dreams, desires, ambitions, and cultural ways of life. We deny we do this, and then we do it. But men did it in the Bible, for example, when they tried to link Jesus with their own nationalistic hopes and dreams; we do it today with our partialities.

One of the disciplines involved in forging a real-world faith is the constant purging of our hidden agendas when they are disclosed. It has been my experience that if I do not engage in this discipline, Christ's Spirit tends to do it for me. And this can sometimes be a painful process.

Could not the avoidance of this process produce a faith that might be considerably smaller in scope and capacity than that Jesus taught in word and deed when He moved among people? I am not making accusations; I am asking questions when I wonder aloud: Would Jesus find Himself comfortable with modern practices of faith? Personally, I find such a speculation very frightening.

St. John tells of a day when thousands gathered to hear Jesus speak. So high was their enthusiasm about the Lord that they were ready to make Him their king. He probably could have said the word that day, and they would have marched en masse to take on the first Roman garrison they could find and start a war with their bare hands. Jesus knew that was their mind-set. He also knew that the faith He was preaching and the faith they were hearing were two different things. Our Lord did what we modern communicators (at least I) would find it difficult to do. He reduced the crowd from several thousand to twelve. And even the dozen or so who remained were shaken.

How did He carry out this public relations reversal? He restated the faith once more in a way that the crowd could not misunderstand.

One can almost hear Jesus saying to them, "I'm not sure that you've heard what I've been saying, so I'm going to walk you through it all again. And when you think you've heard it clearly, if you want to leave, OK. The rest are welcome to stay."

That's what He did. And they left, muttering, "This is a hard teaching. Who can accept it?" The good news was that they had heard the content of Jesus' faith; the bad news was that they didn't accept it when they really heard what He was saying. In terms we hear used on the street today, you could observe that Jesus was not market-driven. Rather, He was commitment-specific. As the crowds dissipated, John describes the Lord turning to the remaining few (His most loyal disciples) and saying, "You do not want to leave too, do you?"

Simon Peter responded, "Lord, to whom shall we go? You have the words of eternal life. We believe and know that you are the Holy One of God" (John 6:60–69).

In other words, Jesus, you're the only One with a boat we're confident won't sink.

The point of the story is that just expressing enthusiasm about Jesus and being part of the crowd that occasionally bids Him be king is not real-world faith of the kind I'm going to attempt to describe. It is an insipid faith that collapses rather quickly under the weight of the reality of God's presence, or the pressure of deep self-discovery, or the challenge of making some personal history that brings about an eternal difference. Some may call it faith, but it isn't!

The smithy pounds on with his hammer. Sometimes he pauses to reheat the metal; sometimes he stops to measure the piece he is reshaping to assure himself that it will match the one it's replacing. And then he pounds again. And even though the strikes of the hammer do seem so wild, each is as carefully aimed and timed as if it was a micromovement of a surgeon cutting on a brain with a laser. The smithy knows what he is forging. And so must the Christ-follower. He or she who wishes a faith for the Heavens, for the inner self, and for the streets must grab a hammer and start pounding.

That may be what St. Paul had in mind when he wrote, "Keep on working with fear and trembling to complete your salvation, because God is always at work in you to make you willing and able to obey his own purpose" (Phil. 2:12–13 TEV).

CHAPTER TWO

Managing Your Real-World Faith

 A Thought for You, Smithy

Forging a faith is your task, Smithy. Don't let visitors, critics, or even friends distract you from your objective. Listen to them when they're helpful, but don't let them define your work.

In early sixteenth-century England a spiritual revolution occurred. It started slowly and then gained momentum when the Bible was first translated from the Latin into the common person's English, "the vulgar tongue."

The English people were held in a kind of spiritual bondage by a medieval Catholic system whose hierarchy enjoyed vast power, principally the power of fear, over the kings and the people. The spiritual revolution, kindled by the English Reformers, overturned that power and gave the people of the streets the opportunity to come to a comprehension of Christ-following faith in the real world by reading and interpreting the Bible for themselves.

The history of that revolution is not always a neat and tidy story, and one's eyebrows continually raise at the antics of people on all sides of the conflict. Nevertheless, there were some remarkable personalities whose courage and focus can inspire every Christ-following generation.

One of the first leaders of the English Reformation was Thomas Bilney. A brilliant young student at Trinity Hall in Cambridge, Bilney was "of serious turn of mind and bashful disposition, and whose tender conscience strove, although ineffectually, to fulfill the com-

mandments of God." Those are the words of an eminent nineteenth-
century historian of the English Reformation, Jean Henri Merle
D'Aubigne, who wrote *The Reformation in England.*

Bilney's attempts to forge his faith under the directorship of various priests failed. No technique, no theology, no human influence
worked, and he became increasingly gloomy. D'Aubigne writes,

> "Alas!" said he with anguish, "my last state is worst than the
> first." From time to time an idea crossed his mind: "May not the
> priests be seeking their own gain, and not the salvation of my
> soul?" But immediately rejecting the rash doubt, he fell back un-
> der the iron hand of the clergy.

Things changed, however, when Bilney's friends introduced him to
a new translation of the New Testament in the Greek language. Before
long he was reading the words of St. Paul: "This is a faithful saying,
and worthy of all acceptation, that Christ Jesus came into the world to
save sinners; of whom I am chief."

"He laid down the book," D'Aubigne writes, "and meditated on
the astonishing declaration . . . he read the verse again and again."
Bilney was simply overwhelmed by the notion that St. Paul would refer
to himself as both a sinner and a person who was saved.

> This declaration continually haunted him, and in this manner God
> instructed him in the secret of his heart. He could not tell what
> had happened to him; it seemed as if a refreshing wind were blow-
> ing over his soul, or as if a rich treasure had been placed in his
> hands. The Holy Spirit took what was Christ's, and announced it
> to him. "I also am like Paul," exclaimed he with emotion, "and
> more than Paul, the greatest of sinners! . . . But Christ saves
> sinners. At last I have heard Jesus."

"Bilney never grew tired of reading his New Testament,"
D'Aubigne writes. "He no longer lent an attentive ear to the teaching
of the [establishment theologians]; he heard Jesus at Capernaum,
Peter in the temple, Paul on Mars' Hill, and felt within himself that
Christ possesses the words of eternal life."

Thomas Bilney went on to be a formidable preacher, a man who
drove the established church mad as it tried to retain its control over

the king and the English peasantry. Finally in desperation, certain of the church officials managed to have him jailed in the Tower of London where he remained for some time.

The story is long and involved, but there came a day when Bilney was put on trial and found guilty of heresy against the church. But the judge, desperate in his desire not to pronounce the automatic sentence of burning at the stake, stalled the procedure for several days, challenging Bilney to think through his faith and consider recanting. Bilney wasn't interested.

Thomas Bilney would never have recanted as a result of the encouragement of the judge or his enemies. But his friends? That was another matter. During the interlude between his conviction and the sentencing, people he liked and trusted visited him in his dungeon, imploring him to do anything that might save his life. Recant and live to preach another day, they counseled. Their "encouragements" were effective, and Bilney permitted them to influence the forging of his faith.

D'Aubigne describes the doubt that began to grow in Bilney's mind—doubt that he was as smart as he thought he was: "His friends who wished to save him, not understanding that [a recanting] Bilney would be Bilney no longer, conjured him with tears to have pity on himself; and by these means his firmness was overcome."

A trusted bishop friend visited him and also pressured him to rethink his decision, and Bilney asked himself: "Can a young soldier like me know the rules of war better than an old soldier . . . ? Or can a poor silly sheep know his way to the fold better than the chief pastor of London?"

As the hours wore on, Bilney's friends would not let up. You can almost feel his spirits sag under the bombardment of their advice as to how he ought to live in this crisis.

> His friends quitted him neither night nor day and, entangled by their fatal affection, he believed at last that he had found a compromise which would set his conscience at rest. "I will preserve my life," he said, "to dedicate it to the Lord." This delusion had scarcely laid hold of his mind before his views were confused, his faith was veiled, the Holy Ghost departed from him, God gave him over to his carnal thoughts and, under the pretext of being useful to Jesus Christ for many years, Bilney disobeyed Him at the

present moment. Being led before the bishops on the morning of Saturday the 7th of December, at nine o'clock, he fell. . . .

. . . and whilst the false friends who had misled him hardly dared raise their eyes, the living church of Christ in England uttered a cry of anguish.

Later a great Reformer of the time, Hugh Latimer, would say to his congregation regarding Bilney's loss of nerve:

"If ever you come in danger, in durance, in prison," said Latimer [another of the Reformers preaching about Bilney to his congregation], "for God's quarrel, I would advise you, above all things, to abjure all your friends, all your friendships; leave not one unabjured. It is they that shall undo you, and not your enemies. It was his very friends that brought Bilney to it."

And so Thomas Bilney recanted, to the delight of the judge and the established church. Within days he was horrified at what he had done, realizing the process that had led to his weak performance.

Thankfully, the story does not end in such an unfortunate way because, when released, Bilney went back to the countryside and began to preach again. But he soon realized that the decision made in the dungeon had been a misguided one and that he had surrendered control over his choices. Living with a sense of shame about his defeat in the shadow of the stake, Bilney determined that if the occasion ever arose again, he would not shrink a second time.

That day did come, but this time, awaiting his execution, the friends who surrounded him were much more mature; they comforted and affirmed him. One of them said to him, "Tomorrow the fire will make you feel its devouring fierceness, but the comfort of God's Holy Spirit will cool it for your everlasting refreshing."

On the night before he died, he amazed his visitors with his extraordinary courage.

I feel that fire by God's ordinance is naturally hot; but yet I am persuaded that when the flames consume me, I shall not feel them. However the stubble of my body shall be wasted by it, a pain for the time is followed by joy unspeakable. . . . "when thou walkest through the fire, thou shalt not be burnt."

"These words remained imprinted on the hearts of some who heard them," D'Aubigne quotes one observer of that evening, "until the day of their death."

The next day Thomas Bilney marched to the stake. He was remarkably composed, obviously in charge of himself. I call it self-mastery. He prayed on his knees, quoted the Apostles' Creed, and publicly confessed his faith in the incarnation and crucifixion of Jesus. The spectators were greatly moved. So much, in fact, that the church leaders feared the people might grow angry at the church's instigation of the execution and withdraw the giving of their alms. Unfortunately, their uneasiness seemed aroused only when it had economic implications.

As he was being tied to the stake, Bilney sensed the crowd's restiveness and spoke, assuring them of his acceptance of events. "Good people," he shouted, "be not angry against these men for my sake; as though they be the authors of my death, it is not they."

And then the fire was lighted, and Bilney slowly died. A strange revolution took place in men's minds after this death: they praised Bilney, and even his persecutors acknowledged his virtues. The bishop of Norwich was heard to exclaim, "I fear I have burnt Abel and let Cain go."

This story out of Christian history has great meaning for me. First, it affirms that a person's faith is initially forged as he or she interacts with the Bible. Second, the story of Thomas Bilney reminds me that our practicing faith can be greatly influenced, if we permit, by the pressures of our opponents *and* our friends. We will most likely never face the terrible decision Bilney had to face when he recanted. But it is significant that external influences began to manage Bilney's faith for him. Left alone, with only the Holy Spirit to prod, he might have maintained his original courage.

Finally, I am impressed with the faulty thinking that led to Bilney's "abort" decision. I'll be useful for more years of preaching, he reasoned. It sounds like the modern Christ-follower who says, "I'll make a lot of money so I can give it to Christian organizations." Or "I would like to be successful in my career so that I will be able to impress people with my witness." Or "we need to live an upscale life so that we can be in touch with wealthy people." Just enough truth mixed with just enough deceit makes for a faith that is not real-world.

In that light, return with me to the shop of the blacksmith where unique things are forged over an open fire.

Using the analogy of the blacksmith and his work to depict the work of faith is nothing new. Scores of poets and authors have done it down through the years. But usually they have depicted God Himself as the Divine Blacksmith and the superheated metal on the anvil as the man or woman being shaped.

One poet, for example, described the sometime painful process in words like these:

> How He hammers him and hurts him,
> And with mighty blows converts him
> Into trial shapes of clay,
> Which only God understands.

I hope I do not cause misunderstanding when I turn the metaphor of the blacksmith about and use it in a slightly different way. But in this book I want to view myself and each individual who shares these words with me *as blacksmiths in our own right: people taking a hard look at what it means to become like Christ (for that is the practical essence of the Christian faith) and managing the process for ourselves as God's Spirit gives wisdom and motivation.* That's what Thomas Bilney of the sixteenth century seems to have learned.

I mean no presumption when I urge a more active self-management of one's faith. I say this because I sense a tendency among too many professed followers of Christ to permit (even invite) others, who seem stronger and smarter (but not necessarily more saintly), to dictate to them what faith, or Christ-following, ought to look like in terms of deeds, perspectives, convictions, routines, and disciplines. I call this *blind* or *undiscriminating followership* (I have manufactured a word).

Blind Followership

When blind followership happens, one unwittingly bows to subtle pressures to be like, talk like, pray like, believe like some very persuasive and sometimes intimidating person who claims to know the answers to just about everything. This unhealthy process, taken to the extreme, moves people into the territory of what is commonly known today as the cultic. You see this possibility in many different circumstances, not just in the religious community but also in other parts of our world. But let me stick with observations germane to the Christ-following movement.

When I was much younger, I was part of a fellowship that included a layman who had an unusual capacity to memorize large portions of Scripture. Many people were greatly impressed with this capacity, and as a result, they attributed to him great wisdom.

Now, the man was a good person, but as I see it now, he was not a wise one. And simply knowing lots of Bible verses by heart did not seem to alter that fact. But more than once I saw well-meaning people retreat before his expressed opinions on many subjects and set their own convictions aside because they perceived him as superior due to his amazing skill in memorization. "Look at how well J—— knows the Bible. Who am I to disagree with him?" each of them would say. In this case people mistakenly assumed that memorized Scripture translated into great insight on a host of other matters.

This possibility of blind followership can be seen today in a much greater scope. Electronic and printed mass media have brought us into the era of the radio and television preacher and the best-selling author. Today the Christ-following community can hear daily or weekly the opinions and judgments of highly gifted communicators who can captivate us with their talent in handling scriptural texts and producing precise interpretations. It is the day of the mass mailing list, the organizational magazine (which is often not open to rebuttal), and the international speaking circuit where a single person operating above serious accountability can exert inordinate influence on how people go about cultivating their knowledge of God and their view of the world.

The best of these offer listeners questions and biblical principles, challenging us to think for ourselves about the most appropriate responses to a saving God and to the issues raging in a dangerous world. They do us a great service.

But the others pepper listeners with all the "answers," leaving little room for disagreement. Purposely or inadvertently, they divide the Christ-following movement and influence people toward inflexibility on issues and perspectives. They build ideological or theological empires that encourage arrogance and pride, the kind St. Paul warned the Corinthians about. In the Protestant tradition it has been standard to decry the Roman Catholic papacy when it claimed inordinate powers to excommunicate and to speak to the church with the authority of divine inspiration. And yet the influence of some Protestant leaders over their followers may actually be stronger in a practical sense than the influence any modern pope ever enjoyed over Catholics.

On a few occasions in my young adult years, I was drawn with mixed results to the influence of such strong persons in the Christ-following movement: those who appeared to have a more powerful command of a certain theology or Greek and Hebrew words, or those who had amazing oratorical ability and could speak without notes, or those whose personal charisma just simply seemed to outshine mine.

On each of those occasions, I found myself trying to bend my personality, my vocabulary, my habit patterns, to be like or to think like that person. I experienced the approval of some people when I did that. But such attempts quickly became empty and dissatisfying, and I found that I was left with a sense of not being true to myself and, to be candid, not really liking myself.

Trying on another person's faith was like wearing another man's suit. If he was a size 46 long, my size-39-regular frame just wasn't comfortable, let alone well draped. I found the same thing in trying to forge a model of faith that was compatible with my psychology, my life-experience, and my mind. I could listen to others and learn. But I could not be their clone.

In the battle of discovering this principle I found new meaning to words that had once profoundly affected St. Augustine when he chose to follow Christ: "Rather, clothe yourselves with the Lord Jesus Christ, and do not think about how to gratify the desires of the sinful nature" (Rom. 13:14). There were "clothes" worth trying on.

Passive Followership

There's another view of faith building that could be just as injurious. Many of us grew up in Christ-following traditions that highly emphasized the notion that God shapes us and our faith. We heard from some sources that if we took a benign or passive position ("just let go and let God"), God, in some strange, mystical way, would do all the necessary formation of faith in us and through us. I call this *passive followership*.

I want to be respectful of the biblical passages where we seem to see God ordering events and circumstances and appearing, at first, to take the management of faith out of a person's hands. And I want to be respectful of those whose teaching leans over backward to highlight

those experiences and suggest that it should be that way for every
Christ-follower.

But there is a confluence of actualities here. It is also quite clear
that God does not call a person to suspend the intellect, the emotions,
or the personality when he sets off to follow Christ. God does not call
a person to sit on his hands or become a puppet. Does one submit
intellect, emotions, and personality to the Lord for further refinement
and development? Certainly! But pretend that they have no relevance
to what I will become as a Christ-follower? Never!

When Joseph of the Older Testament first talked with his brothers
about their treacherous treatment of him years earlier, he told them,
"You intended to harm me, but God intended it for good" (Gen.
50:20). Out of insights like that has come our understanding of the
marvelous doctrine of God's providence: the summary truth about a
God who operates in time and space to bring people and events, the
best and worst of both, together for the greater good of His long-range
design. I believe that doctrine more forcefully today than ever before.

But I do not believe that doctrine implies passivity as a spiritual
lifestyle. Nor does it mean waiting around and letting events take their
course. Rather, I see the doctrine of God's providence paralleling the
freedom the Lord gives to a person to set a course of Christ-following
that walks right into reality and masters it. Take charge: measure the
events about you; inventory your capacities; make choices, take risks,
and watch what happens.

I am drawn to the way I see Joseph aggressively engaging his world
and pursuing excellence, effectiveness, and opportunity as a slave, as
a prisoner, and then as the chief administrator of the Egyptian government. How Joseph's personal initiative was networked with God's initiative is a mystery I am not likely to resolve this side of Heaven. But
my inability to fully comprehend the tension does not discourage me
from following Joseph's example.

Joseph, like others I will want to point out, appears to have assumed a *proactive* (a modern term I love for *initiative*) perspective on
life. He refused to lie down and let events roll over him. He reminds
me of a sports team that always has to play on the opponent's field
before a hostile crowd but rejects the possibility of losing or settling
for a tie.

Joseph was tough, flexible, consistent, and fair. In slang terms,
there were no wimp factors about him. People ended up playing by his
rules. And he won: relationally, vocationally, and spiritually. The faith

he forged—his hold on God; his mastery of himself; his interpretation and handling of current events—was right on target.

Like Joseph, it is ours to take what God reveals to us and to forge a faith experience out of it.

We must *own* our style of Christ-following; it must fit us and make sense in the private and public worlds in which we operate. It cannot be relevant on the weekends and irrelevant on weekdays. Forging this faith is work, a noble work, and no one can do it for us. Help us? Sure! Do it all for us? Never!

Somewhere Thomas Bilney may be saying, "Hear! Hear!"

CHAPTER THREE

Stick Close and Follow Me

A Thought for You, Smithy

*Faith isn't always pounded out in the most con-
venient places or under the most ideal circumstances, Smithy. Your sweat, your calloused
hands, and your dirty apron make it clear that
you're working hard. But faith is not formed in
comfortable places; only at the anvil where things
are often tough.*

What the h—— is this thing about accepting Christ?" he asked me. "I can't relate to that language at all."

"We're talking about a relationship," I responded. "It's personal and dynamic and likely to be life-altering."

"Well, that's another matter. But I don't understand how that could begin by accepting Christ. I can't think of any relationship that goes very far by just accepting a person. I mean, I accept you. That simply means I'm willing to let you be you and not make a big deal out of it. And I hope you accept me. But then what? Where do things go from there? So accepting Christ doesn't make much sense to me."

"Then how about 'following Christ'?" I asked. "You know that when He connected with people, Jesus' most frequent personal invitation was simply, 'Follow Me.' Apparently, they knew exactly what that meant because it was a familiar invitation on the part of teachers. In practical terms it meant living with the man for a while and learning to look at all of reality the way He saw it."

"That's an improvement. I can see some sense in that concept. And it certainly makes it clear as to who's on top and in the lead."

"That was probably the point when Jesus gave His invitation to follow. He was challenging people to change the direction in which they were walking through life and switch to the direction He was walking. It meant acknowledging that they needed forgiveness for previously walking the wrong way, that they needed to convert His teaching into a way of life for themselves, and ultimately that they would tell other people what they'd discovered in their continuing journey with Christ.

"You might be interested to know," I went on, "that in many cultures, those who call themselves Christ-followers today speak of the Christian life as walking the Jesus-road or doing things the Jesus-way. It seems far more descriptive than the way we talk about it in English."

He responded, "So you're saying that accepting Christ and following Christ are the same thing. Why don't you call yourself a Christ-follower then? That's a much better description than Christian or born-again Christian. Who knows what any of that stuff means anymore?"

The day that conversation happened I switched over to Christ-following as an apt term for what I chose to do when I first made a decision to forge a real-world faith. And the day that conversation happened I reminded myself that I can get so used to certain words that I don't realize the words become meaningless after a while. They are like algebraic symbols, x's and y's, which mean something only if you know what the assigned values are. But don't expect anyone to understand your private x's and y's.

How we follow Christ, what we become, and what happens as a result are among the practical issues involved in forging a real-world faith. If we choose to hammer out a style of Christ-following that is highly limited, restricted to "in-house" religious activity alone, our faith becomes dwarfed, unreal, relatively useless. We adapt to a private vocabulary that becomes comprehensible for everyone inside the circle but becomes gibberish to those outside the circle. Eventually, we fall out of touch with those outside when it comes to matters of Christ-following faith.

Over the years, I have observed that long-term Christ-followers have relatively few friendships of influence with those outside the community of faith. Many acquaintances with neighbors or working associates? Yes. But acquaintances of influence? No. What has happened? Adopting an "inside" lifestyle, using a vocabulary known only to those inside, and being reluctant to engage in the issues that usually interest "outsiders," the average Christ-follower can effectively cut himself off from making a substantial contribution to his generation.

My first indication of how a faith can lose touch with the real world came when I was a boy in public school. The son of a minister, I spent large parts of my weekends in church. There, because I was the pastor's son and because I had managed to master large amounts of Bible information, I was somehow a very popular person. In fact, socially speaking, I was king of the mountain with all the churchgoing young people.

But on Sunday night I went home in a virtual state of gloom. Because from Monday morning until Friday evening I was what they now call a nerd. Every week cycled like that: on the top on the weekends; on the bottom during the weekdays. The memory of the pain of that early divergence of lifestyles has remained with me until this day. Later on, I came to realize that I had permitted myself as a boy to be "bicultural" in my lifestyle. Somehow I knew how to master subcultural patterns of Christ-following on the weekends; but I was a stranger to the rest of the world on the weekdays. I had not learned to be conversant and comfortable in the larger context.

That difficult period of my life gave me a picture of what many men and women must experience today as they too attempt to pursue a Christ-following life. If they have not come to understand that following Christ leads straight toward the streets and not just toward the church, their faith will not be of the real-world variety. Instead, they will develop a language and lifestyle that fits the weekends, and an alternative language and lifestyle (sometimes recessive; sometimes duplistic) for the weekdays.

In most of the American states with colonial roots, there are organizations dedicated to the preservation of the memory of the colonial militias. When meeting or appearing in ceremonial functions, the members wear the uniforms and carry the muskets of former times. They fire blank charges from their cannons and generally make a lot of noise and smoke. It is very impressive.

But these militiamen would never go off to modern war dressed or equipped in this way. In real war, real bullets fly, and soldiers fight for keeps. There are real casualties and real victories.

Real-world faith may enjoy the ceremony on the parade ground (or in the church building), but it is designed to perform best in the battle where the "bullets" fly. Real-world faith takes on real missions, real issues, and real opportunities. And it knows that there will be casualties and victories.

Today I have come to understand that to follow Christ through life is to "drive" (as moderns like to say) all my relationships (from intimate to distant), all my moral and ethical values, the management of all my assets, my career choices, my perspective on struggle, pleasure and pain, and my ultimate view of life, death, and afterlife on the basis of what He has said and done as a precedent and assume that this is what it means to please God, my Maker. Obviously, that is no small matter.

As I implied, some people are quite comfortable following Christ through the world of the church and in the company of people who are similarly connected. And some extend Christ-following beyond the church into their home and friendly environments where Christ's values are either honored or at least tolerated.

In a biography of Senator Robert Kennedy, Lester and Irene David describe an unusually hot New York spring day in 1968 when Kennedy was furiously fighting for the Democratic nomination for the presidency. For five hours he crisscrossed streets in some of the poorest neighborhoods in Spanish Harlem. By the time the tour was ended, Kennedy was caked with dirt and soaked in perspiration.

His guide that day was Jose Torres, the former world's light heavyweight boxing champion.

> Ever since Bobby had announced his candidacy for the Presidency, Torres had wondered why the rich man's son came to the ghettos on quick trips back east; why, in fact, he was working so hard and so long, often sixteen hours every day, for a goal that seemed so distant for him. At the car, Torres asked, "Why are you doing this? Why are you running?"
>
> Bobby replied in a voice so low Jose had to lean close to catch the words.
>
> "Because I found out something I never knew," Kennedy told him. "I found out that my world was not the real world." *(Bobby Kennedy: The Making of a Folk Hero)*

It has to be said (and said over and over again) in the spirit of Kennedy's words: the church and the fenced-in ground of the religious organization or program are not the real world either. The forging of faith may be taught there, but faith is designed to be implemented beyond there. And that is what Christ wants to do: lead us beyond the ground of the religious and out into places that often seem strange or frightening.

Recently, Gail and I drove to a small community to be part of a dinner. We had never been there before, and we were quickly lost. Seeing a policeman parked in his car, I pulled over and asked him for directions, something I hate to do.

"You go down two more lights; turn right and go to a fork in the road where you bear left. Go two stop signs . . . or is it three. . . . No! Here's an easier way. Make a U-turn and go back to that little shopping mall back there; you know the one with the gas station on the corner. You hear what I'm saying? Turn left there and just follow the road down to the ocean. It makes several turns, OK? And you have to be careful not to. . . . No! Go back to the first way I said. Go down. . . . Oh, what the heck. Look, I'll take you there. Just follow me, and stick close!"

I followed him and stuck close. And it occurred to me along the way that that is the invitation of Christ to someone who wants to know God, figure out the inner self, and understand how to live in the real world. Follow Him and stick close. Christ doesn't miss a turn.

And when you follow Him and stick close, where does He lead?

I hear Him first invite the follower into a place I am going to call the HEAVENLIES, the "place" where God is and where a new behavior is called for. There one learns the importance and the activity of worship, a function I once thought to be relatively impractical. *That place called the Heavenlies is the real world.*

Then Christ invites the follower to tail after Him as He enters the cavernous depths of the INNERMOST BEING of a person where the scenery is not always attractive to behold and where there is need for constant exploration and renovation. When I'm that traveler, I don't mind the first few feet of the journey, but then I begin to get cold feet.

I'm reminded of the day, years ago, when we took our two preschoolers into Mammoth Cave in Kentucky. They quickly informed me that they preferred the daylight, and the intensity of their feelings about the cave increased when the guide turned off the lights. If Christ did not make it clear that following Him requires this descent into self, I for one would never go beyond merely looking down the first staircase. *That place called the innermost being of a person is the real world.*

And finally, Christ proposes to take the lead when the follower enters the PUBLIC SQUARE OF THE WORLD where people like myself work and learn and play and do awesome things, good and bad, beautiful and ugly, constructive and destructive.

This walk through the streets is itself an eye-opener. *But the streets and all the places they lead to are the real world, and the faith we are forging gets its greatest workout in the streets.* To be on those streets is to know the language of the streets, the dangers and seductions of the streets, the beauty of the streets, the needs and possibilities of the streets.

I walk through a stockbrokerage house in midtown Manhattan as the guest of a private investor in the firm. A hundred people or more are hunched over computer terminals, their eyes glazed as they scan the numbers that tell them what is going on at the world's stock exchanges. They mutter facts over phones to institutional and individual buyers and sellers, hoping to win a buy or sell order that will produce a commission. The place is a madhouse, and my host quips, "Be careful. You're standing knee-deep in greed."

I ask myself, How is Christ followed here? In this place where money is made from money and the word crash is the ultimate profanity, would He seek employment here? And if He did, how would He handle the pressure? And what would His reaction be like when a customer called and claimed that he'd been cheated out of a buck? Can you see Christ encouraging a client to enter into a stock deal that is ripening toward a buy-out, and a two-for-one split? How would He handle the temptations of insider trading? The Bible does say something about Christ's being thoroughly intimate with all forms of temptation. But how does that take shape in the forging of a real-world faith?

I stand in the middle of a subway almost crushed by the rush-hour crowd that knows no dignity as people press up against one another. Better to be squeezed than to wait for another train. Tempers are short; odors are strong; discourtesy abounds. When the doors open at the next stop, one young woman turns to the man behind her and shouts at him, "You know; you're a real jerk." Had she assumed that his hands were where they shouldn't have been? He shrugs his shoulders and starts to protest that he hasn't done a thing.

She doesn't wait for his response, however; she disappears into the swirl of commuters on the platform. And I ask myself, How is Christ followed in this atmosphere? Would He have apologized if falsely accused of jostling a passenger? Would He have tried to explain Himself? Or would He have ignored her like so many New Yorkers would? Would Christ even come here? Is He here? Does He know anything about the commuter's world? The Bible says that He is always with us. What does that mean? The answer has to be part of my real-world faith.

A man lies in a grotesque position on the front steps of our church building in Manhattan. Several empty bottles are lying in disorder around him. Is he sleeping off a drunken state? Did he fall and seriously injure himself? What would he do if one were to shake and awaken him? Start fighting? Become abusive? What does he need?

Standing there, I ask myself, How is Christ followed in this situation? Would He call 911? Would He let the man sleep it off? Would He take the chance of getting clubbed when He offered a helping hand? Now, let's be honest, does Christ love this person, and does He know him as intimately as I've been taught to think He knows and loves me? In fact, does He feel the same way about every person on this street? I know the biblical answer; but something dark within me has a rough time with it, and that has to be hammered out in the forging of my real-world faith.

In a burst of enthusiasm, I pay out more money than I care to admit to purchase two tickets to a Broadway musical for my wife, Gail, and me. We sit that evening in a magnificent theater and listen to music and see dancing and laugh at jokes that are the epitome of professional entertainment. We wince a bit at some of the occasionally off-color humor and grimace when a dancer appears in a costume that is a bit too scanty for our sensibilities.

This is a crazy situation. Paying a high price for an entertainment experience that at one moment is an aesthetic delight and at another an embarrassment over things you like to think you stand for. And in my bewilderment I ask myself, How is Christ followed in a place like this? (Right out the door, I hear someone answer.) I'm not so sure. But it's a fair question. Would He ever sit and laugh at a comedian? Would He take the time to listen to a song? Would He purchase a theater ticket? Was He there in the audience that night? If He was, how did He handle the situation? The struggle is part of forging a real-world faith. The trading room of the stockbrokerage house, the subway in rush hour, the steps outside a building where a pathetic man lies, and the glitzy theater with its brassy music are parts of what I call the real world. No one plays games here. The air is competitive, harsh, painful, and bottom-line oriented, whatever that line may be.

No one talks about love, caring, or the joys of fellowship. If someone does, it seems to come across as corny. This is where humanity spends most of its waking hours: where life is difficult, often sad, frequently painful, and usually unjust. Where is Christ in all of this? How does He view these scenes? Does He avoid them, or does He invade them? What is His comfort level in such surroundings? I would really like to know because I have to walk through places like these all the time and so do others I know. How do I follow Him as I make history in these places?

And knowing how to do this is what real-world faith is all about. It takes sweat, tears, thought, and prayer. It is being forged—pounded out—on a regular basis.

Malcolm Muggeridge writes of a time when he escorted Mother Teresa into a New York television studio so that she could be interviewed on a network morning show, "a program," he writes, "which helps Americans from coast to coast to munch their breakfast cereal and gulp down their breakfast coffee." He goes on to say that her interviewer was a man "with a drooping green mustache, a purple nose and scarlet hair."

> It was the first time Mother Teresa had been in an American television studio, and so she was quite unprepared for the constant interruptions for commercials. As it happened, surely as a result of divine intervention, all the commercials that particular morning were to do with different varieties of package food, recommended as being non-fattening and non-nourishing. Mother Teresa looked at them with a kind of wonder, her own constant preoccupation being, of course, to find the wherewithal to nourish the starving and put some flesh on human skeletons. It took some little time for the irony of the situation to strike her. When it did, she remarked in a perfect audible voice: "I see that Christ is needed in television studios." A total silence descended on all present, and I fully expected the lights to go out and the floor manager to drop dead. Reality had momentarily intruded into one of the media's mills of fantasy—an unprecedented occurrence. *(Christ and the Media)*

This is what happens when someone follows Christ into the streets and sees things His way. Who follows Him there?

There is no world that this Christ does not know. The "world" of the Heavenlies, the "world" of inner space, the "world" of, well, the world. And He has apparently called men and women to follow Him through these worlds, watch Him act, and form themselves similarly. That's what it means to take one's life, put it on the anvil, and rigorously hammer it into shape—Christlike shape.

And this book is dedicated to the notion of thinking about what it takes to do that.

CHAPTER FOUR

Case Study: Muddy Moments and a Real-World Faith

A Thought for You, Smithy

Smithy, this faith you're forging can't snap the minute it meets stress. The world has seen the shabbier stuff that's produced on assembly lines: cheap materials and shoddy workmanship. Determine to make something that endures under all situations.

It had rained for several October days in New Hampshire, and our dirt road—a narrow passage through the woods to our Peace Ledge home—was a strip of mud. But just how muddy it had become was not apparent until Bill, the local cement-and-gravel man, drove onto the property with his dump truck loaded with sand and crushed rock I'd ordered early that morning. My intentions for the day had included some improvement on our driveway.

But that wasn't going to happen—on that day, anyway—because the eight rear, weight-bearing wheels on Bill's truck suddenly sank to the axles in the saturated ground. It didn't take long for Bill to conclude that he wasn't going to go any farther, and so he turned off the engine, climbed down from the cab, and stood for a moment looking quietly at the undignified posture of his vehicle.

Moments later he broke his silence. Like most taciturn, rural New Englanders, Bill frequently expresses his deeper feelings through the use of a special, somewhat limited, vocabulary of nouns and adjectives. In this case he used only one of those words, a monosyllabic

44

one. But when Bill used it (and I've heard him use it often), it came out as if it contained two syllables. Although the word is only four letters long, it took Bill several seconds to complete its pronunciation. And when he repeated it in the same way several more times, I knew exactly what he thought about my mud and his stupidity for not fore-seeing what was likely to happen on a dirt road after all that rain.

Then, seeming to remember that I did not make it a habit to use the word he had just spoken, he turned and gave me a sheepish grin and mumbled an apology. Anxieties expressed, we began to study how we could pull the truck with its heavy load from the mud since every hour that it remained motionless would cost Bill significant business revenue. And when we had a plan, we moved into motion.

First, we off-loaded the rock and sand to lighten the weight on the wheels. Then we drove in my pickup to Bill's gravel pit, loaded his bulldozer on a flatbed, and returned to the site of the stranded dump truck. Bill, now confident that we would quickly have the problem solved, attached the ends of a chain to the back of the Caterpillar and to the front of the truck. He revved up the dozer's diesel engine and started to pull. I stood off to one side and watched as the chain became taut and began to bear the strain of the tug-of-war between raw horse-power and New Hampshire mud.

The mud won!

The problem wasn't with the bulldozer; it was certainly adequate. But the chain wasn't. It couldn't take the strain put on it. Good for some things, Bill's chain simply didn't measure up to this task. It broke as if it were a piece of string. Three times Bill used the remain-ing length of chain to pull on the front of the truck, and three times the chain snapped. With each failure, Bill expanded further on the vocabu-lary reserved for stressful situations. And he no longer bothered to apologize.

Obviously, we needed a heavier chain: one that matched the de-mands of the situation. And only when we returned to the gravel pit and found one, did we get the job done. As I noted, the bulldozer's power was more than adequate, and with the chain of greater strength, it quickly prevailed over the mud. The dump truck obedi-ently came forth.

For a long time after Bill, his dump truck, and his bulldozer had left Peace Ledge that day, I pondered the events that had taken place on the muddy road and speculated on how it all reflected issues that often agitate down in the deeper places of my inner being. You must understand that I am a broodish sort of person who spends large amounts of time in my inner space. I've come to realize that I live far more within than I do in the outer, more public world. So it would not be unusual for me to take an event—such as a truck's getting stuck axle-deep in mud—and seek a more profound message that might help me to understand my private world.

What kept sounding within me was the plight of that dump truck. It was a picture, I thought, of me (and not a few others) in life's darker moments: those times when one feels trapped in the mud of difficult questions and choices, or murky circumstances and painful consequences in life. I'm thinking of times when there is fear, dread, intimidation, or doubt; when there is a numbing sense of loneliness, insignificance, or apathy. Perhaps you could call those times, common to all of us, the muddy moments of personal experience.

Surely all of us must have muddy moments. Some of us are more ready to admit to them than are others. Your muddy moments may differ from mine, but regardless of their variances, they are just as real to each of us when we get bogged down. Metaphorically speaking, when muddy moments come, we are likely to spin our "wheels," exhaust our "fuel," put wear on our "engines," and sometimes seem to get nowhere. Have I stretched the image too far? It would be nice to think that one could go through life without ever getting axle-deep in muddy moments. But given our blind spots and rebel-prone spirits, given the unpredictability of other people's choices that will have untold rippling effects, and given the random consequences of evil in our world, some muddy moments are a certainty for each of us and should be anticipated.

As a businessman, Bill, the cement-and-gravel man, was realistic; he anticipated muddy moments in his business. And that's part of the reason he kept chains in his shed at the gravel pit. He had to be prepared to pull his machinery out of holes like the one at Peace Ledge. And when one chain couldn't do the job, he had another one that did. He would have been a naive truck driver if he'd trusted in his "luck" to keep out of muddy holes. No, he knew that he couldn't go out and make a buck if he wasn't willing to take some risks that might eventuate in muddy moments. The chains were there to use when that happened.

Like many others, I have spent a lifetime developing a view of life in this world that reminds me of that chain. I call my view of life *my faith;* it's my version of reality. I think of my faith as something like

Bill's chains when I regularly ask myself, Is my faith capable of standing up under the tension that goes between power and problem? Does it reach far enough? Does it hold when the mud is the deepest? A person's faith is not made exclusively for muddy moments, naturally, but in those times of extreme duress a person's faith is put to the severest tests and shown to be adequate and realistic or not.

Real chains, of course, are comprised of links. At the foundry each one is forged with the anticipation that it will stand up under an anticipated amount of stress. Some tiny chains are designed to support only a locket or a medal about a person's neck. Some chains are designed to constrain a prisoner. And some are made for lugging heavy logs out of a forest. The heavier chains I've seen are used to raise ships' anchors from the floor of the harbor and pull heavy-duty dump trucks out of muddy holes.

You don't want a necklace-strength chain to lift an anchor. And of course, you don't need a chain made for a ship to put around a person's neck. You do want a chain with links forged to face up to the demands of the situation.

At each stage of my life I have needed a faith that not only made sense in the peak moments of success but also brought hope and new starts in muddy moments of failure. I have sought a faith capable of helping me acknowledge that I am really a very plain person who will never be special in terms of wealth, heroism, or brilliance but who is nevertheless special and valuable in the eyes of the One who put the spark of life in me.

When I think about real-world faith in history and the people who provide the best models, my mind swings to Daniel of the Older Testament who served four kings in the court at Babylon. In reading Daniel's life story, most readers will skip over a brief but significant phrase at the end of the first chapter of the book summarizing his story: "And Daniel remained [or lasted] there until the first year of King Cyrus" (Dan. 1:21).

In a world like ours where one may sell his or her career many times over during a lifetime of work, it is useful to take a serious look at a man who started at or near the top and stayed there for decades. He lasted! Like a well-conditioned runner, he started the race and finished it strong. His was a style of faith like Bill's second chain. It was made up of links forged to bear up under any situation. And that's why Daniel will pop up all over this book. If anyone owns a real-world faith, Daniel is it!

Anyone who went to Sunday school feels familiar with Daniel because the great stories of his career in the king's court were related so regularly. In my Sunday school we sang songs and colored pictures featuring Daniel's great moments. We even used our imaginations to dramatize his moments of personal crises (I was usually a lion).

Actually, the Bible reader has only the record of four or five significant incidents in Daniel's professional life and a smattering of details about his personal life. There are large gaps in his resume, years and years about which we know nothing except that he was consistently successful and that his bosses could not have been more pleased with his managerial performance. It is clear that no one could find a scintilla of sleaze in any sector of government where Daniel was in charge.

The administrations in which Daniel served were not kind, benevolent nonprofit institutions where the growth and the development of people were put before achievement of task. On the contrary, Daniel spent a lifetime in a working culture where brutality and callous indifference for the welfare of people (except as they served the interests of the throne) were the order of the day. Slavery was condoned; human life was extended or forfeited at the whim of a king; POWER—absolute, Machiavellian in scope, emanating from the point of a spear—was everything.

Not only did Daniel live in that sort of world virtually all his life, but he did business at the very top echelons of its system. The very fact that he did so and that the story is told in the Bible is a message in itself. We who identify with the theological tradition of biblical authority and who believe that God inspired the process of authorship and providentially watched over the compilation of the biblical literature might want to ask some questions. What was God trying to get the reader to think about when the story of Daniel was included? How did this man manage to bring God such great pleasure? One might be tempted to wonder why God didn't lift such a gifted person as Daniel out of such a hideous workplace. Are there modern Daniels working in such diverse places as Wall Street or Fleet Street, the Kremlin or the KGB, Hollywood or Las Vegas, Shell Oil or Panasonic? I was just wondering. Maybe one would spot them only after a lifetime accumulation of decisions and activities.

When we study the lives of great men and women, it might be wiser if we first studied the world in which they lived and the challenges they were likely to face before we assess the qualities of the person. Daniel is a case in point. Having heard his story so often, I am tempted to think of this man as a kind, faithful, even quiet type who showed up on the scene and interpreted a dream or two and then backed off until he was summoned again.

But the facts are quite different. The man went to work every day. He managed large parts of one of the greatest political establishments that has ever existed. One can only guess at how many people he governed and how much power he wielded. One can only imagine how quick he had to be on his feet to decode a culture in which he had not been born. It all suggests someone who had to be smart, politically astute, tough, persuasive, and impervious to intimidation, bribe, or graft. Credit Daniel with the ability to adjust to the shifts in political winds as different kings moved onto Babylon's and later the Persian throne. Daniel was a survivor and a "thriver."

Other things can be said about Daniel's world. It was marked with enormous human suffering and oppression. Human existence was viewed as cheap in value, and the life of an individual or an entire local population could be snuffed out at the king's word. Even government officials could lose their heads if their actions hinted at disloyalty or incompetence. One had to have something of the spirit of an alley fighter to function in a world like that.

Furthermore, Daniel had to work in tandem with men whose operating policies were utterly abominable in terms of the values and laws of his God. Wealth was accumulated through war and confiscation, and some grew rich while others were impoverished. He had to move in a political world in which people seeking influence played the "games" of intrigue. Daniel was almost victimized by persons who were jealous of his achievements who tried to manipulate affairs so that his life would end in the lions' den.

If I worked for a major corporation or a massive governmental enterprise, or if I found myself in a business known for its inclination to dishonesty or exploitation, or if I worked alongside people whose motivations were decidedly hostile to the interests of the God of the Bible, I'd want to get to know Daniel well. I'd want to brood on the parallels between his work situation and mine and whether or not he often left his work exhausted by the drain on his spirit as might happen to me. I'd want to know if he ever had to address problems that had no simple or obvious solutions. And I'd want to know how he did it.

It is likely to make some of us uncomfortable, but we may have to face the truth that Daniel would not have survived as long as he did if he had not been willing to negotiate lots of compromises on issues that must have greatly bothered him. But to get something positive done, he must have had to accept trade-offs that eventuated in consequences he quietly abhorred.

His job was not for a person with a brittle point of view. His inner spirit must have been beaten up again and again as he saw how impossible it was to take a stand on every issue that came across his desk. He must have spent hours and hours thinking through how to reserve the use of his "clout" for those moments when an issue of paramount significance arose. He chose the moments well because when they came (and he chose only a key few), Daniel used his influence with consummate skill, and everyone, including the king, backed off rather quickly.

When Daniel went to work each day, the king got his money's worth. What Daniel did, he did excellently. He was the best there was. He worked hard; he worked smart; and he worked for the "company," advancing its interests—not necessarily *his* own career—putting his foot down only when he saw issues that dramatically conflicted with the macro-interests of his God. And in those times others learned that they would have to answer to Daniel.

When the man chose to blow the whistle (as we have become fond of saying here in America), he seems to have chosen landmark situations: the moral conduct of a king and his ruthless policies concerning captive people; the translation and application of a message on the wall, which foretold the collapse of a regime; the issue of religious freedom and a king's Satan-like defiance of God's sovereignty. When pressed to the test on each of these matters, Daniel never wavered; he took the offensive and charged.

You would never find Daniel taking the advice of someone who had considerable experience in a world where no one played by the rules and the competition took no prisoners: "When in charge, ponder; when in trouble, delegate; when in doubt, mumble." That wasn't Daniel's style!

When he faced the sneaky investigative activities of members of the opposition party who were jealous of his success, he emerged impeccably clean from the ordeal.

The conclusion of his critics? "We will never find any basis for charges against this man Daniel unless it has something to do with the law of his God" (Dan. 6:5).

To the extent that they had read the situation accurately, credit Daniel's enemies with intelligence. And that is why it was not long before laws were passed that were designed to drive a wedge between the sitting king and his faithful colleague. It became an unnerving test of Daniel's real-world faith. Could it remain consistent in its disciplines when civil law said that all worship not directed toward the king should cease? Could it stand the pressure of a show trial? Could this faith produce courage when events suggested that a lifetime of career building was about to be dissolved? Could it work in a den of hungry lions? Was it really a faith for the real world?

Answer: yes. Daniel had a version of reality that was operative in the offices at the top, in the privacy of his bedroom where he knelt to intercede with God three times a day, and in a lions' den. And when he walked out of there the next morning and appeared before a shaken king, the faith was working just as powerfully, for the man was as cool as he had ever been. That is real-world faith.

Is it an understatement to say the obvious? Daniel lived in a real world of life and death, intrigue and ambition, success and failure, stress and pressure, winner-take-all competitions. He never walked away from it no matter how dirty and seamy it seemed to become. It was as if God said, "This is a vile and arrogant system human beings have created. I want a few faithful people in the middle of it to represent My interests and to be agents of both restraint and influence when it is necessary." It should be noted that God never lifted Daniel out of that real world. Instead He made it possible for Daniel to forge and employ a faith that made him fit for every situation.

My friend Edward England, who graciously publishes my books in England, once wrote a delightful book, *The Unfading Vision,* which was a special encouragement to me. In it he quotes Dietrich Bonhoeffer who said shortly before his death in the real world of a German prison camp: "It is only by living completely in this world that one learns to have faith. . . . By this worldliness I mean living unreservedly in life's duties, problems, successes and failures, experiences and perplexities."

And Daniel seemed to do it that way. He never ran. He stayed at the forge and kept hammering even when the heat was oppressive and the task seemed impossible.

There is a chain fit for every situation. When my friend Bill needed one, it was ready, hanging in his shed. For too many years I—and more than a few like me—have been too comfortable with versions of reality that, like lightweight chains, are only useful for the good times. But life, as I have painfully discovered, has its muddy moments. And if there is not a chain whose links are forged with the intention of providing maximum performance, the mud might win. A faith that is not real-world tested might have the same problem.

THE REAL WORLD
OF THE HEAVENLIES

To follow Christ is to meet God

in the real world of the Heavenlies

and

give Him the best gift

a human being can give

and that is worship

CHAPTER FIVE

The Steel Ladder

 A Thought for You, Smithy
The quality and determination of your labor,
Smithy, will be only as strong as your vision of
the One who commissioned your work. If your
esteem for Him is unbounded, no effort will be
too great in seeking His pleasure.

For more than forty years I have retained a childhood memory of an obscure place in the church building where my parents took me to Sunday school and worship. At the rear of the sanctuary in a small room called the usher's closet, there was a steel ladder bolted to the wall. It reached upward to a locked trapdoor in the ceiling.

That trapdoor opened to a small balcony above the sanctuary's rear doors. I had no idea what was up there, and no adult thought it important to inform me. The result? A mystery that could not be resolved because children were strictly forbidden to climb the ladder. Only later would I learn, with disappointment, that the balcony was merely a storage place for old Christmas pageant scenery, obsolete church records, and an undetermined number of dustballs.

But I didn't yet know that when I was three, maybe four years old, and my unsatisfied curiosity about the balcony went wild. What was really up there that no one would tell us about? In the absence of better information, I came to the conclusion all on my own that God lived up there and that the balcony was . . . well . . . probably Heaven.

When individuals, no matter what their age, begin thinking like this, they are beginning to form a *theology,* a word that intimidates a lot of people. My theology wasn't difficult to devise. It simply emerged from childhood speculations.

55

For example, grown-ups often discussed "talking with the Lord"; I overheard them telling one another about how "the Lord had led them" or how "the Lord had spoken to them."

When might things like the Lord's "leading" or "speaking to" people happen? And where? The answer? Simple! The big people in my world had a key to that trapdoor, I reasoned, and when children were in bed, they (the grown-ups) ascended the ladder and talked with God. I assumed that this was one more example of the many things adults were keeping from children. In this case they guarded their secret by simply invoking the right to forbid us to climb the ladder ourselves.

But that was not the end of my theological inventions. I conceived a picture of the God living at the top of the steel ladder, who, when the congregation was meeting in the sanctuary, would stand and raise up His arms in a patriarchal pose much like one I'd seen in a painting of a giant shepherd standing among a flock of sheep.

But, I also theorized, He would stand and raise His arms only if everyone's eyes were closed. Otherwise God remained hidden behind the partition at the balcony's edge. This thought helped me to make sense of why people closed their eyes while praying.

I had plenty of time (and I mean plenty of time according to a child's scale of time) to think these things through during interminable sermons. I wondered, for example, if one could ever catch God off guard and sneak a glimpse of Him before He realized that not everyone's eyes were closed.

I thought a lot about this and pondered the possibility that, were I successful, I might be severely punished. Wasn't there something in the story of Moses about people not being able to look at God?

But I decided to take a chance, and during a long pastoral prayer one morning, I slowly, painfully, inched myself around to a peeking position. But before I could get a line of sight, God was gone. God knows everything, someone had said, so it came to me that He had been aware of my intention long before I even started to move.

That meant only one other possibility: surprise. Could one swing about so quickly that God could not disappear in time? Perhaps His reaction time was a bit slow. I tried the sudden swivel just once to the consternation of my mother who wondered at this convulsive movement and why it happened at prayertime. But she never received an explanation from me as to what I had been thinking. If she and my father were going to keep their secrets about the balcony, I was going to keep mine.

A few times on weekdays I tried peeking through a door in the front of the sanctuary when I knew it was empty. But the God of my imagination always managed to foresee when I was going to do this and either ducked or disappeared before I could see Him. I finally accepted the fact that the God who lived at the top of the steel ladder could not be tricked.

It occurred to me to wonder what God did in the balcony, and I concluded that only three major things might interest Him. One: He monitored the church services for personal purposes. Two: He apparently managed the weather. Three: He granted exclusive interviews to grown-ups who had a key to the trapdoor.

Such was the "balcony theology" of a three- or four-year-old. If there is any significance to those childish speculations, it is in the fact that they were the efforts of a person, however infantile, to know some facts about God and to deal with His existence in the best way possible. Examine this rudimentary perception of God I once constructed, and you will see that some of the basic notions that people identify with God were actually there. The god of the balcony was mysterious; he knew some things I didn't know; he was more powerful (at least quicker); and he was present and intimate (at least with adults).

The misperceptions? I was clearly confused about what the Bible means in saying that the Lord God of Heaven and earth is Spirit and therefore invisible (as we perceive material visibility). I was obviously off a bit on the location of Heaven and what it was like. And finally, I missed it when I reasoned that God limits Himself to adults at the expense of children (of course, the disciples of Jesus were not far from believing this).

This last misperception—that God had no time for children—may have been the sad one. But it was understandable in light of the fact that, as a child, I often heard from adults that children should be seen and not heard. Perhaps God also felt that way?

What else can be said about my theology of a God at the top of a steel ladder beyond that it was a remarkably faulty view? Only this: this God was too small, as J. B. Phillips once put it; He was impotent and trivial. A lot of people may smile at my early grasp of God, but the fact is, their theology may not be much better. Theirs also may be a vision of a God who is too small, too impotent, and too trivial. And so Phillips wrote:

> The trouble with many people today is that they have not found a God big enough for modern needs. While their experience of life has grown in a score of directions, and their mental horizons have been expanded to the point of bewilderment by world events and by scientific discoveries, their ideas of God have remained largely static. It is obviously impossible for an adult to worship the conception of God that exists in the mind of a child of Sunday School age, unless he is prepared to deny his own experience of life. If, by a great effort of will, he does do this he will always be secretly afraid lest some new truth may expose the juvenility of his faith.
> *(Your God Is Too Small)*

Such pitiful theologies are the primary cause, the root, of an innocuous faith, which when employed to deal with the real self within and the real world without simply can't do the job.

It is a dangerous thing—a very dangerous thing—to have a skimpy impression of the Almighty God. But that is the state of millions upon millions of people whose perspective of the Creator and His purposes is so puny that He has become virtually the last thing they respect or fear. Pardon the candor of my opinion if I suggest that many of the millions who so misjudge God attend church every Sunday.

This paltry view of the Almighty is not merely an intellectual matter. As I said a paragraph or two ago, it has direct linkage with our subsequent life-performance in the real world and our exploration of ourselves. I have come to realize with great sadness that, in my own experience, the most costly sins I have committed came at a time when I briefly suspended my reverence for God. In such a moment I quietly (and insanely) concluded that God didn't care and most likely wouldn't intervene were I to risk the violation of one of His commandments. Among the things I have learned from this is that good theology today, not carefully maintained, can become sour theology tomorrow. And sour theology begets the possibility of destructive behavior.

Where does this lead? Let me put it in a way I have never heard it put before. I believe we need to cultivate a sense of following Christ into Heaven where God the Father dwells. And what does one do there? Form a personal theology, a vision of God. Who is our "tour guide"? Jesus. And what do we learn? How to worship. And what difference does all this make? *It is the first of three phases in the forging of a real-world faith.*

One day Jesus led three of His disciples toward Heaven. They got as far as the top of a mountain, where a spectacular scene unfolded. In a blaze of glory, Jesus conversed with Older Testament saints about his own reentrance to Heaven. One of the three spectators, Simon Peter, later wrote of what he had experienced. It is clear from what he wrote that this moment marked him for the rest of his life. And although the implications of it all took a bit of time to sink down deep into his soul, the job got done. For Peter's long-range faith took on stamina and force that made him formidable in his real world. What had Peter seen?

> We have not depended on made-up stories in making known to you the mighty coming of our Lord Jesus Christ. With our own eyes we saw his greatness. We were there when he was given honor and glory by God the Father, when the voice came to him from the Supreme Glory, saying "This is my own dear Son, with whom I am pleased!" We ourselves heard this voice coming from heaven, when we were with him on the holy mountain (2 Pet. 1:16–18 TEV).

I sense that, although he didn't know it at the time, Peter's personal theology took a long leap forward on that mountain. As he would later look back on those events, he would come to realize that reality was a lot larger than what one saw with the eyes or heard with the ears. There was immense power in the Heavenlies and a hint of it had bathed that mountaintop. One had no choice but to live in great reverence of it. Only now was Peter's vision of God prepared to expand.

In his book, *The Knowledge of the Holy,* A. W. Tozer writes,

> What comes into our minds when we think about God is the most important thing about us.
>
> The history of mankind will probably show that no people has ever risen above its religion, and man's spiritual history will positively demonstrate that no religion has ever been greater than its idea of God. Worship is pure or base as the worshiper entertains high or low thoughts of God.
>
> For this reason the gravest question before the Church is

always God Himself, and the most portentous fact about any man is not what he at a given time may say or do, but *what he in his deep heart conceives God to be like*. (Emphasis mine)

A real-world faith, interestingly enough, begins then not with a sorting of issues on earth but with an exploration of the Heavenly places to gain a true view of God and how one acts in His presence. Again, it isn't usually said this way, but *to follow Christ means to follow Him FIRST into the presence of His Father and to learn how to properly act there*.

In her book, *Walking on Water,* Madeleine L'Engle quotes Alice Kaholusana, a Hawaiian Christ-follower:

Before the missionaries came [to Hawaii], my people used to sit outside their temples for a long time meditating and preparing themselves before entering. Then they would virtually creep to the altar to offer their petitions and afterwards would again sit a long time outside, this time to "breathe life" into their prayers. The Christians, when they came, just got up, uttered a few sentences, said AMEN and were done. For that reason my people called them "haoles," [people] "without breath," or those who failed to breathe life into their prayers.

When I first read Ms. Kaholusana's words, I recorded them in my journal with a prayer of my own: *Lord, forgive the times I have actually barged into Your presence without a thought to my conduct. Like the "haoles," I have often come breathless before You and have left with no breath in my prayers. Inexcusable!*

I spent my three years of high school two thousand miles away from home in a private boarding school. Weekends were often lonely because most of the students who lived within a reasonable distance went home. My roommate's home was not far away, so I usually received an invitation to join him. His was a lovely home on the ocean, and his family provided a warm welcome each time I visited. My friend's father often handed me a five-dollar bill when we walked through the door. "Gordon," he would say, "when you live in our home, you spend our money."

I loved that home away from home. I always looked forward to going there (for more than just the five-dollar bill). And as I have looked back on that unusual hospitality, I have pondered its likeness to what Jesus seems to say to any person who makes a choice to respond to Him. "Follow Me," I hear Him say, "and I will take you home to meet My Father. You'll get to know Him well if you come after Me."

He said that very thing as He pondered the more permanent visit the people of God will one day make in the presence of God: "I am going there to prepare a place for you. And if I go and prepare a place for you, I will come back and take you to be with me that you also may be where I am" (John 14:2–3).

When we follow Christ into the Heavenlies, we enter into the life-long process of meeting God.

> Meeting God: living with an awareness that He made us, that He searched us out through Christ when we were disinterested runaways, that He energizes us, that He is intimately conscious of our existence, and that He loves us enough to draw us to Himself.

To this day I am incredulous when I think about meeting this God or His having a loving curiosity for knowing me. Of all the great questions that one might ask Him, I wish to know how He could be constantly aware of every human being with equal, affectionate interest. Often as I walk the streets of New York City and look upon the faces of innumerable people of every station in life, I wish to ask God, Do You really have knowledge of every one of these as I like to think You have knowledge of me?

A few years ago I read of a young Florida man who became devoted to Elvis Presley before he died—*and* after. For Dennis Wise, devotion meant spending every bit of money he had to collect Presley memorabilia (books, magazines, pillows, records, and even tree leaves from the Presley mansion in Memphis). Devotion also meant that Wise underwent six hours of plastic surgery to make his face resemble that of the famous singer.

But having collected all this stuff and having attempted to look like him, did Dennis Wise ever meet Presley when he was alive? No, he told an interviewer. He'd seen him perform several times, and he had once seen him at a distance when he looked through the gates at Graceland (Presley's home). He had stood there for more than twelve hours to get a fleeting glimpse, and that is all it was: a glimpse. With all of his devotion, Dennis Wise never got to meet his idol.

When I read this interview, I realized that Wise had done just about everything one does when he worships a god. Learn what you can;

assume what similarity you can; meet him if you can. Problem: Dennis Wise's god was unknowable, and he is now dead. And that takes care of whatever chance there used to be of a personal encounter.

The God to whom Jesus introduces us is not dead, nor is He unknowable. And that is the great genius of Christ-following faith.

And this is where real-world faith begins: when we meet God and expand the capacity of our inner spirits and our minds to appreciate His infinite majesty and glory. A lifetime of single-minded searching concerning who God is and what we can know about Him would hardly scratch the surface of all the possibilities. But that search is the most noble of all tasks.

The Older Testament prophet, Jeremiah, was dealing with this issue when he presented the voice of God as saying,

> The Lord says: Let not the wise man bask in his wisdom, nor the mighty man in his might, nor the rich man in his riches. Let them boast in this alone: That they truly know me, and understand that I am the Lord of justice and of righteousness whose love is steadfast; and that I love to be this way (Jer. 9:23–24 TLB).

Was that written more than twenty-five hundred years ago or last month? Perhaps times have changed, but not the issues. Western man as a rule still seems to bask in the values of brilliance, power, and wealth. And here comes this man, Jeremiah, who says that this trilogy of values so long revered among human beings does not really count in the Heavenlies when compared to a greater issue. Which is? Meeting and knowing God. Again, it's the key to a real-world faith.

Some people may be bothered that anyone is eligible to meet and know God. Anyone! Gender, race, IQ, family heritage, alma mater, age, bank balance, and notoriety are not significant matters when it comes to knowing and meeting God. There are no entry fees, no hoops to jump through, no social connections, and no initiation periods. Anyone can meet Him. Unfortunately, a relative few make the effort. Thus, few possess a real-world faith.

Daniel understood this priority value. Hardly anyone in his generation could have rightfully basked in wealth, power, and wisdom more than he could. But he wasn't interested in that kind of basking. What really drove him was the pursuit of a knowledge of the God of Heaven from both an academic and a personal perspective. That knowledge made it possible for him to negotiate his way through a tough and complex world. It was certainly the blessing of his real-world faith.

The first major crisis in Daniel's career erupted when his boss, King Nebuchadnezzar, had a disturbing dream. Since most of us aren't dream-driven today, we're not likely to get too overwrought about somebody's nightmare. But in ancient times a monarch's bad dream set off shock waves throughout a royal court until someone put the king's mind at ease with a soothing interpretation. Tell the man what he wants to hear must have been the interpreter's motto. In this case, however, either the king had forgotten the details of the dream and retained only the bad feelings it had produced, or he knew what the dream was about and wasn't telling.

Either way, it was a test for the dream experts because, before they could decode the message of the dream, they had to describe it. This apparently was hard to do, and before long, Nebuchadnezzar was in a state of apoplexy because no one could do the job. A departmental death sentence was pronounced; a purge was on. And it would have been carried out except that Daniel stepped forward and made an appointment with the king to resolve the problem.

Daniel's first thought was to join his three companions in a prayer as he prepared for his meeting. The text of the man's prayer is stunning. Every phrase shows why Daniel would never cower before a mere emperor. One who prays this kind of prayer has met a great God: a God so great that the universe itself is hardly big enough to contain His glory. When you pray to a God like this, every other issue is small potatoes. This is definitely not a God who lives in church balconies.

> Blessed be the name of God forever and ever, for he alone has all wisdom and all power. World events are under his control. He removes kings and sets others on their thrones. He gives wise men their wisdom, and scholars their intelligence. He reveals profound mysteries beyond man's understanding. He knows all hidden things, for he is light, and darkness is no obstacle to him. I thank you and praise you, O God of my fathers, for you have given me wisdom and glowing health, and now, even this vision of the king's dream, and the understanding of what it means (Dan. 2:20–23 TLB).

The tale of the emperor who had no clothes features a small boy at curbside during a parade who was innocent and uninhibited enough to say what everyone else was thinking but afraid to admit. The emperor was naked; and the kid said so. Are children and clowns the only ones who speak the truth to kings who have the power of life and death over their subjects?

Men and women with a theology like Daniel's would probably speak the truth to kings. Not because they are innocent or a bit crazy, but because they have a greater reverence for a greater sovereign: not a god at the top of a steel ladder, but the God of Heaven and earth. This theme of people conversant with the glory of the God of Heaven and earth and their resulting courageous living in the real world is a prevalent theme throughout the Bible.

What did they all have in common? A faith that operated under real-world conditions. They faced down human powers, laughed in the presence of death threats, and sneered at the seductions of temporary profit. Why? Because first they had met God and learned how to act in His presence.

It has been forty-five years since I stood at the base of that steel ladder and longed to take a peek through the locked trap door. And the day finally came sometime after I had abandoned my ridiculous notions about God living up there. "Go ahead," someone had said when the door was unlocked, "climb up and take a look." I did. As I said before, I saw only junk.

What a deflating experience after all that former speculation! But it would be a lot worse to know that one had walked through life and quaked in fear or bowed in subjugation to all the wrong things, like corporate boards, nasty bosses, social pressure, financial security, or death itself. Then to discover that these were only "gods" who lived in dusty balconies and really were in the final analysis far too small and too trivial. They were emperors without clothes.

Jeremiah: to know and understand me . . . that I am God. The Christ who calls us to follow invites us to follow Him home where He promises an introduction to His and our Father. That's when real-world faith begins to get forged.

CHAPTER SIX

God Is Multilingual

A Thought for You, Smithy
Faith can take different shapes under the hands
of different smithies. So when you see others do-
ing a similar work, don't be tempted to copy
them. Enjoy contrasts; celebrate differences;
learn from the masters. But let your work reflect
what you were made to be.

A few years ago I had an experience that left me internally unraveled for a short while. The distress began at the conclusion of a conference I attended for a small group of nonprofit organizational leaders.

For three days, participants had offered and responded to presentations on a theme of mutual professional interest. It had been a rewarding set of meetings, I thought, as we came toward the last scheduled function, and I was glad that I had been included on the invitation list.

The speaker for the final session was considered by many to be a veteran spokesperson for the evangelical Christian movement. As he walked to the podium, I think most of us anticipated a scholarly and insightful summary of our deliberations.

But that didn't happen. Soon after he began, it became clear that he was perturbed over what he had been hearing for the past three days, and that he felt a general rebuke was in order. He was angry, he said, and he felt obligated to use his senior position among us to express his dismay. Most of us sat frozen to our chairs, not daring to move.

I am usually put off by angry people, but this time did seem different. Something deep within me sensed a rightness in what the man was saying; his harsh words cut deeply and exposed within me a certain shallowness of spirit.

Soon, I found myself weeping in response to his words, and I wondered if this was not a moment similar to those ancient times when a Jeremiah or an Isaiah spoke. Was this how it sounded when they excoriated the people of their generation for shoddy thinking and insipid faith? I began to feel that I was witnessing a powerful revelation of God's Spirit. I recall thinking that we were meeting God through this message in a way that would leave all of us changed. That was *my* enthusiastic hunch about what was happening.

When the powerful speech was concluded, I knelt. A few others did also. And for the better part of an hour we joined in a circle of prayer that was as intense as anything I had ever experienced. Again, I had no doubt: God was in that room, and I was aware of His holy presence.

A few hours after that stirring time, I boarded a homeward-bound airplane and shared a three-seat section with two other conference participants. They were much older and considerably more experienced men than I was, and I counted heavily on their judgments. I guess I was hoping that one of them would reflect on that last hour and say, "We have waited a lifetime for a breakthrough like this."

So when we were belted into our seats, I popped my question. "How did you feel about that last meeting? Has anything like that ever happened before?"

As I remember the conversation, it went on from there like this:

"How did I feel?" the first responded. "I was repelled. I couldn't wait to get out of there. I was so disgusted I could hardly contain myself. You know, he's flown off the handle like that several times before."

"That's the way I felt," the second added. "I don't know why R—— [the moderator of the conference] didn't see that coming and find a way to preempt it. We didn't need that at all."

That's when my unraveling began.

"You didn't sense anything of God's movement upon the people in that room?" I asked the two. I was dumbfounded over their words. "You didn't think that what was said needed to be heard?"

"Not really. I thought it was a cheap shot, an insult to all of us, if you want my opinion."

It took a long time for me to get over that airborne exchange. In short order I flip-flopped, believing at first that God had powerfully spoken and then reaching an opposite conclusion: all I had really heard was the emotional outburst of an old man trying to have a last word and gain attention for himself. *How could I trust my judgment when these two "wise men," with their long-time experience in these sorts of things, saw things differently?*

My spirit was in chaos. Should I trust the original impulse of my spiritual instincts? For, as I noted, something had responded within me as I'd listened that morning. Or should I go with the evaluations of others who were older, smarter, and better connected than I was? Sadly, easily influenced, I moved toward the latter alternative. And I concluded that God hadn't really spoken at all.

The Bible teaches—in fact it high-profiles—a Creator who speaks, who has made Himself accessible to human beings much like a benevolent king, an equitable judge, and a tender father. The Bible makes it clear that it is possible to meet and to know God on a personal basis. Remember Jeremiah as he made short shrift of those who bask in claims of life-success as denoted in terms of wealth, power, or intelligence. "Let a person bask in this: that he understands and knows God," Jeremiah said.

Jesus was insistent about how this process happens. "No one comes to the Father but through Me," He said. Add this to the many such things He said about knowing God, and you get a strong impression of where real-world faith begins and develops its expansive energy: Christ escorts us, if we follow, into the presence of His Heavenly Father.

So if a Christ-follower follows the Son of God into the Heavenlies, how does he come to understand and know the Father? The experience that day simply reenergized this question that had turned over and over within me for many years. It was a question I could not seem to satisfactorily answer in spite of my years of experience in the Christ-following tradition.

Just as in this case at the conference, in other confusing moments I concluded that my timing or my sensitivity was off. Those were times when I thought nothing was happening and then later concluded that God must have been doing something and I missed out on it. There were also times when I thought something extraordinary was happening and later decided that nothing had happened. I know I am not alone when I confess that on many occasions, I was absolutely sure that I knew what God was saying or doing only to wind up in dreadful, paralyzing uncertainty just a few days later. Frustrating!

And that kind of frustration is not alleviated when one meets someone who never admits to a doubt about these things. Some men and women speak with an unnerving confidence that they have heard God clearly on a matter. They know what's right for themselves in items of truth and activity, and they know what's right for everyone else. They leave their audiences or followers with little choice.

A lot of years passed in which I quietly struggled with the notion that I must be something of a second-class Christ-follower in comparison to those who seem to have easy access to Heaven and who come away each time to confidently inform the rest of us as to what He is saying. Sometimes I had a mental image of being in the back row of a crowd following a physically visible Jesus, and all I could ever see of Him was the back of His head as He conversed with those in the front row. In that impression I was always straining to pick up occasional phrases and words and having to depend on the messages passed back as to what the Lord was saying and where we were being led. I could hear myself frequently calling to those up front, "What did He say? What did He mean by that? Where's He going now?" And who knows how distorted the relayed reports were by the time they got to people like me in the back row?

It's not fun having that kind of spiritual self-image. But I know that is something of the impression many, many Christ-followers have about their position in the crowd. They are back there where I once thought myself to be (which is not to say that I have lately placed myself near the front). Yet how many would admit to having this sort of self-image? Answer: a lot of people in their quiet, darkened moments when nothing is working and God seems to be a million miles away. Sometimes it seems as if I meet one of them every day.

Perhaps you can understand now why an experience such as the one I had at that conference could become so upsetting. I thought that a breakthrough had occurred for me, that I had come to the front of the crowd. For once I had witnessed and been caught up in a marvelous thing. But then in my uncertainty I permitted some others to impeach the significance of the moment. I was plunged back into my quiet uncertainty.

I am much older now: the same age, I suspect, as one of the two on the plane that day. Now I know that I should have weighed their opinions more carefully, and I also know that what happened in that conference room was probably a move of God's Spirit after all. Whether it was as dramatic a matter as I thought at first, I don't know.

The point is, I live now with a greater confidence about these things than I had then.

I will probably continue to wrestle with the question—how does God speak to me and how do I speak to Him?—for the rest of my life. But now I know that one reason I struggled with this issue of meeting God then is that I am naturally disposed to commune with Him in certain ways and under certain circumstances. And the ways and circumstances are often different from those of others.

In other words, the conditions in which Christ-followers most naturally send and receive "signals" to God are diverse, and we cannot make the mistake of prescribing any single way as best for all. This simple conclusion has brought me much personal relief. And by the way, it is a conclusion that may irritate some Christian "gurus" who like to design a single uniform method of Heavenly approach for everyone.

As I have monitored my journey as a Christ-follower and as I have watched many others moving in the same direction, I have observed that each of us has what I would like to call a *leading instinct of the soul*. This leading instinct is the way of sending and receiving "signals" to God that we most frequently employ when we want to engage in sacred or spiritual activity, when we wish to know and understand Him better (Jeremiah's words).

This leading instinct is something like a spiritual language for us, and when we are able to speak it and be with others who speak this same language, we are at ease and most comfortable. Conversely, when we are among people who speak a different language of the inner spirit, we may have a certain sense of discomfort, even a kind of spiritual culture shock. We long to get back to where we can more easily sense God's activity and make more confident judgments about it.

I used to think that when I was among Christ-followers who spoke a different spiritual language as we sought to meet God (and I am speaking figuratively), one of our languages had to be in error. More than once I observed the confidence of those "speaking" the other way, and I assumed it must be me because I wasn't as sure as they seemed to be. This is so sad, and I belabor this point because I think many Christ-followers suffer from this same suspicion.

I have a memory of a visit I made to another country where I was the guest of a family who lived there. They did their best to offer me unrestrained hospitality. But in spite of their efforts I found myself becoming literally homesick, melancholy about how long it would be until I would return home.

The host family literally spoke a language I could not understand, and I had to rely on their occasional translations into English about what they were saying to one another. They conversed loudly with one another in their mother tongue, and they underscored their incomprehensible words with what seemed to be wild gestures. Every bit of intuition I had said they were all angry. But they weren't! It was their cultural way of expressing themselves. They loved one another as much as the members of my family loved one another.

The family did strange things—at least strange to me. They ate at late night hours; I was used to eating in the late afternoon. They ate slowly; I ate swiftly. They loved to be together in one small room; an introvert, I loved to be alone. They made noise; I needed quiet. The contrasts abounded.

Nevertheless, the difference in literal and cultural languages notwithstanding, many of the relational values I thought to be important were present in that family: affection, communication, teamwork, mutual growth, and commitment. But their instincts for expressing them were different from mine, and I received inaccurate signals at first. If I'd trusted my initial impressions, I would have gone home and told my family that I'd been among people who were likely to kill one another. But the situation was just the opposite.

This is an exaggerated example of how we can misjudge the way fellow Christ-followers choose to meet and worship in the Father's presence. Our differing spiritual cultures and languages may tempt us to look upon others' attempts at reverence and conclude that they have much to learn and that they'd be smarter (and more theologically correct) if they would do things as *we* do them. And then we are shocked when we discover that they could possibly feel the same about us.

Knowing our leading spiritual instinct and those of others can be important to our enjoyment of God and our appreciation of the diversity in the Christ-following family. Whether we are born with this leading instinct or it is acquired, I don't know. I simply observe its presence in myself and in others.

Not a few of us will possess more than one of these instincts; additionally, some of us will find one or two of the so-called instincts a bit unpalatable, even unattractive. When we see someone engaged with God in one of the ways that tends to repel us, we may even find ourselves asking, How can God bear to be addressed in that way, or how can that person imagine that he is actually involved in sacred activity?

A fascinating story in the book of 2 Samuel tells of the day King David brought the ark of God to the City of David. He was clearly rapturous by the significance of this moment, and we read, "David, wearing a linen ephod, danced before the LORD with all his might, while he and the entire house of Israel brought up the ark of the LORD with shouts and the sound of the trumpets" (6:14–15). (When we were teenagers, those of us who grew up in churches where dancing was frowned upon loved to call this section of Scripture to the attention of our elders. They were never moved. Those of the charismatic Christ-following tradition love to call this section to the attention of noncharismatic Christ-followers. Somehow it doesn't seem to change minds in this context either. Apparently, when you're convinced, you're convinced!)

The point I raise when I picture David, beside himself with joy dancing in something akin to his underwear (or less), is that Michal, his wife, was utterly repelled by his actions and told him so. She accused him of squandering his dignity. David found her criticism unacceptable and informed her that he would celebrate in whatever way he felt his instincts of the spirit leading him to express himself. The Bible indicates that Michal had no business questioning David's spontaneous worship, and she was judged for her reaction.

I have observed six leading instincts of the inner spirit, six languages if you please. Each seems to have an agenda, a theme of expression, that attaches itself to one of the aspects or attributes of God's being. Thus when Christ-followers of each of these leading instincts follow the Son of God into the presence of the Father, they are most likely to express themselves in one of these languages and come back again and again to this particular agenda.

There is no priority order in the listing of these "instincts." But because something has to be first, I'll select the one I call the aesthetic instinct.

I. The Aesthetic Instinct

The Agenda Is Majesty

Here is a Christ-follower who is most alive within himself when worship, both personal and corporate, is accomplished in an environment of beauty, order, tradition, and artistic integrity. The way things look and sound and connect is very, very important.

The Christ-follower with an aesthetic instinct feels most comfortable in worship that happens in an environment architecturally designed for that purpose. The symbols of the sanctuary—the way it was built and decorated—its ambience, its immensity, its quiet, and its uniqueness in contrast to all other buildings are important. An altar, a special place where Christ is perceived as unusually present, is considered a piece of holy ground. And it is here that the aesthetic Christ-follower finds it easiest to meet God.

The aesthetic Christ-follower wants to employ words that connect with other generations of Christ-followers. Thus, he is drawn to prayers whose subject matter has stood the test of time. He loves the theologically correct creeds affirmed for a millennia or more, and he searches for musical forms of hymnody and anthem that have been affirmed as the best that musicians and poets can produce.

We are describing a person who seeks to be overwhelmed and impressed by the majesty and infinitude of God, and he most experiences it in the context of artistic and liturgical excellence. You will hear him say that he seeks an experience that speaks to the mind as well as the spirit. He is most at ease when dignity, solemnity, and nobility are present in all that happens.

This is most likely a person who is slow to speak out spontaneously or even individually. He is skeptical of those who say that one should "pray from the heart" and not from the prayer book. It worries him that some people sing songs or talk about God and Jesus in terms that seem presumptuously familiar or overly sentimental. He finds it difficult to think of God merely as a buddy who walks and talks (as a song once put it) as "good friends often do."

A list of aesthetic Christ-followers might include David, the great king of Israel, despite my earlier introduction of him as a dancer in a public display of worship. David appears to have been quite artistically oriented. Many of his psalms were apparently written to be sung as part of a liturgical hymnody in the worship center at Jerusalem. Other psalms were actually written prayers, designed to be spoken under rather formal circumstances. There is repetition of words and phrases, for example, antiphonal constructions where two or more choirs tossed great statements of praise back and forth. Some psalms are what we might call litanies, which celebrate God's great acts of power and mercy. They are meant to be spoken aloud in concert by members of the congregation as they meet God.

Perhaps David's greatest aesthetic dream was the erection of a temple, a dream he could not realize but only pass on to his son, Solomon, since God restrained him from doing it. He could not live with the fact that he lived in a beautiful palace but there was no place of superior quality set aside in which to celebrate the presence of God. Thus, his lofty intention of which God approved.

David did everything he could do to get the temple-building project under way short of digging the first hole in the ground. The construction phase was to be under Solomon's direction. David's mandate to Solomon and the people was this:

> Now devote your heart and soul to seeking the LORD your God. Begin to build the sanctuary of the LORD God, so that you may bring the ark of the covenant of the LORD and the sacred articles belonging to God into the temple that will be built for the Name of the LORD (1 Chron. 22:19–20).

Whenever I hear someone express criticism of those who love great classical religious music, liturgies, and the magnificence of a great cathedral, I think I would like to introduce that person to David. I think he would have loved some of the special places and artistic ways in which some Christ-followers of our time meet God. This appears to have been David's leading spiritual instinct, his "language" by which he entered into God's presence and met with Him.

But let me remind you: this is not to say that David wasn't capable of powerful bursts of joyful enthusiasm. Remember this writer of great and formal statements about God dancing that day, delirious with joy, in front of the ark of the covenant. David was a weeper, a laugher, a frowner. He had a wide range of spiritual instincts, and he appears to have thoroughly enjoyed meeting God—at least in those times when he had done nothing stupid.

It's clear that words and structures and music that were skillfully and thoughtfully shaped were large parts of David's perception of how to meet the Father. David was a king, and he understood how kings were to be treated. God was the King above all kings. If David was accustomed to people showing him appropriate homage when they entered his presence in the palace, how much more should David's God receive homage when one or more people entered His presence in the Heavenlies.

Because of David's leading aesthetic instinct of the soul, generations of men and women have met God through the psalmist's way of expressing the joy of understanding and knowing God.

People with an aesthetic instinct enter into the presence of God with great solemnity. And as they kneel in the presence of a God of majesty, they do so with a quiet assurance deep in their souls that God leads with an aesthetic instinct too. But they never tell anybody that they believe this.

II. The Experiential Instinct

The Agenda Is Joy

Appearing to be diametrically opposed to the aesthete is someone I call an experientialist. I'm thinking of a Christ-follower who wants to "feel" the presence of God when he meets Him and to respond with the full range of emotions and even physical expression. Thus, an unaffected clapping of hands, stomping of feet, and even dancing; singing and praying with unbridled enthusiasm, weeping and laughing. There may be a word from God that wasn't prepared in an office lined with books; an expression of praise or prayer in a language no one understands for the moment but whose very sounds are marked with obvious joy.

Not everyone is at home in such an atmosphere. Who is likely to be repelled by this "outrageous" display of emotion? Could be the very same person who acts with even greater passion when his kid hits a home run to win a Little League ball game on Saturday morning.

The experientialist finds it a bit difficult to understand why the aesthete would like to read prayers from an old book when he can meet God and talk to Him in his own street language. And if the street language fails to do the job of sending and receiving signals from Heaven, the experientialist is glad to use other languages and tongues.

Why be "dignified" when the gospel is a hilarious experience? he asks. Why work so hard to plan things in rigid structure when the Spirit of God will give you the right words to speak when the time comes? Why give over the leadership of a worship service to a limited few when everyone ought to have a say in how God is to be spoken to and heard from?

If the aesthete is caught up in the majesty of God as King and Lord, the experientialist is most responsive to the Holy Spirit and the energy He promises to give. A key word in the experientialist's vocabulary is *power*, and that power can be expressed in the healing of persons, the giving of truth directly from Heaven, and the bonding together of people in harmonious relationships.

One of the most interesting and commendable things about the way in which experientialists meet God is the cross-cultural, multi-ethnic context in which it is often done. Of all the leading instincts of the spirit this one seems to bind people of diverse races and cultures the most powerfully.

In a general sort of way, the experientialist and the aesthete are opposites as they seek to meet God. And yet it is not unusual to see them cross the lines of their spiritual preferences and embrace something of the other (for example, charismatic Episcopalians and Catholics). What may be happening here is the discovery that the heart needs both the soul of the experientialist and the body of the aesthete. Interesting!

If David would have spent his time with the aesthetes, I think Simon Peter would have gravitated toward the experientialists. Peter was always a very physical man, an enthusiastic person. He threw himself into things, and he didn't always think first. It's Peter who quickly speaks out to affirm Christ as the Son of God (good news), and it's Peter who, in his love for the Lord, rebukes Him for talking about such morose things as a cross (bad news).

It's Peter who wants to walk on water to be with Jesus; it's Peter who would like to stay on the mountaintop and build altars. And it's Peter who makes bold commitments to stand fast, yet he panics before anyone else and thus makes a fool of himself. With Peter, what you see is what you get—great energy, great intentions, great motion. He loved the Lord as much as anyone could have. No one could have put him into any kind of controlled situation except Jesus.

I don't want to be unfair to the big fisherman, but I have a hunch that Peter, had he lived among us today, would have been put off by a great pipe organ but drawn to an electric guitar and a tambourine. Whatever the man did, he did with feeling—right or wrong—and that's the way experientialists do things.

The experientialist is bighearted and generous. And he seizes almost any opportunity to meet God because there is no doubt in his mind that God is—when you get to the bottom of things—an experientialist too.

There are four other possible leading instincts of the inner spirit of the Christ-follower; they follow in the next chapters. And when we

follow Christ into the Heavenlies to meet God, we may be more comfortable worshiping him in one of those ways. One of the six will leap
out of us, and each of us will be inclined to say, "that's me!" And one
or more will impress us as totally uninteresting.

I think that a growing Christ-follower knows his "language" but
sets out to know all the others too. It makes for a great time when we
follow Christ home to meet His Father.

CHAPTER SEVEN

Builders and Brooders

A Thought for You, Smithy
Some smithies forge their faith in ceaseless activity. Others work alone, in quiet and unhurried deliberation. Watch them closely; they have something to teach you.

Leading instincts or languages of the spirit are the possible ways in which we send and receive signals when we meet with God. Jesus' desire is to lead Christ-followers into His Father's presence. And how do we act when we get there? Here are two more possibilities, and like the aesthetic and the experiential instincts, they seem initially to be poles apart from each other. First, let's consider the activist instinct.

III. The Activist Instinct

The Agenda Is Achievement

The activist sees all of Christ-following activity as service. He is the mega-achiever of the Christ-following family because he perceives God as an achiever. And when he meets with God, he expects the agenda to focus largely on achievement. ("Only what's done for Christ will last," we sometimes hear.) The activist wants to worship by communing with God about good things that need to get done.

We're speaking of a person who is driven by compassion for the disadvantaged, or by prophetic anger against oppression, or by a strong sense of urgency that many people in this world have yet to discover Christ's invitation to follow Him.

77

He sees the world in desperate need of change, and he's committed to changing it. He reads the lives of men and women who were activists and is thrilled by their stories of courage and sacrifice. He finds it energizing to talk about great faith, which is the groundwork for miracles. The activist cannot be content with business as usual; he wants to be a part of extraordinary things. The word *vision* crops up frequently in his speech.

What do activists do? They build bigger churches, contact everyone in big cities, distribute vast amounts of Christian literature, raise huge amounts of money to feed the hungry, picket places they perceive to be evil, train and mobilize large numbers of people to do something they believe to be of eternal significance. The list of potential activities capturing the imagination of activists is endless. But all of it amounts to one thing: get something done that fits into the missionary purposes of Heaven.

Activists read the Bible through a very special lens. They take God's call to Moses and the prophets very seriously. They note Jesus' progressive envisioning of His disciples with the "Great Commission." They study the early life of the church and gain great motivation from the first Christ-followers' remarkable penetration of the world with the story of Jesus. They are entranced by the rapidity with which the church expanded in that day, and they ask why that cannot happen now. And thanks to the activists, that is exactly what is happening in some parts of the world today.

The activist does indeed appreciate the aesthete's message: God is majestic and worthy of high worship. And the activist certainly understands the experientialist's cry of joy and call for power. But he sometimes wonders when the aesthete is going to leave his sanctuary and get busy and when the experientialist is going to realize that the Lord's joy and power aren't just to make us feel good and enthusiastic but to make us capable of getting the work of the kingdom done.

The activist is most comfortable in his faith when he is making plans and projections, when he is mobilizing people and seeing programs unfold. He makes measurements of accomplishment, not because he wants credit (I hope) but because he wants to celebrate what has been accomplished and plan for what else is left undone. When he meets God in the Heavenlies, he wants to have achievements to give as his act of worship. And when he meets God, he wants to talk about the blanketing of cities with the gospel or the blanketing of chilled people with . . . well . . . blankets because he believes that most interests God.

Activists can be either evangelistic or politically and socially involved. Activists can be entrepreneurial, building large organizations or creating strategies designed to spiritually influence specific groups, such as businesspeople, military officers, or professional athletes.

And as you might expect, activists love to connect with other activists . . . if their visions are compatible, of course. They like to confer with one another (the more global in scope the conferences, the better) and read papers on strategies, techniques, and goals of activity. Sometimes they pray together, but they hope that praying will eventuate in action. The world of activists is all very exciting and sometimes even productive if all the plans and programs actually translate into kingdom-building effectiveness.

All of us admire activists because they get things done for God. They may generate a bit of guilt for those who are not as inclined to be that focused. But a little bit of guilt never hurt anyone, and so activists are significant members of the Christ-following family.

The Bible has more than a few activists. I'll pick Moses as an example because I think that was where his heart was. Raw activism got him into a bit of trouble—as activism does sometimes—when he moved a bit impulsively one day and killed an Egyptian guard. He thought that his actions would impress the Hebrew slaves and gain him a following. But that was not to be, and Moses found himself leaving town for the desert as a fugitive. He was gone for forty years while God balanced his leading instinct of the spirit with a bit of opportunity for contemplation. And the man that emerged was a reasonably balanced person in these matters.

But again, at heart he was a get-things-done kind of man. Burned a bit by the Egypt experience? Most likely. He probably would never have returned to Egypt if God had not "jump started" him at the burning bush. But when he swung into action, he pursued the old vision of liberation like a terrier. Only a few times did he get discouraged and paralyzed. But when the Promised Land began to dominate his mental horizon, he never stopped.

Moses was everywhere—playing administrator, adjudicator, and negotiator between God and the people. That he held up under this strain is remarkable in itself. When his father-in-law, Jethro, came for a visit, he immediately saw through Moses' wild activism. "The thing you're doing isn't good," Jethro told him, and he helped his son-in-law restructure things in such a way as to redistribute the load of authority a bit more evenly.

One senses that activist Christianity may be an American contribution to the world Christian scene. The "can-do" mentality of American culture has affected the church and tempted some people to think that sheer determination, hard work, and sacrifice can move mountains.

On the dark side, the activist is likely to experience exhaustion or, as Moses did in his early years, to assume that any means leads toward a beneficial end. The landscape of the Christian community is littered with burned-out activists: those who have lost their marriages or destroyed their own health; those who have been disillusioned when expectations were not reached; and those who met certain goals and then wondered why they were not more satisfied with the results. The probability is that in many cases, an imbalance in the leading instincts of the spirit occurred, and one did not stop long enough to recognize that God can be heard and spoken to in other ways. In short, the activist usually needs to be reminded that when one follows Christ to meet God, the agenda is more than just achievement.

But blessed be the activist. When he goes to meet God—if he has time—he can speak of great missionary exploits, people fed, governments confronted, and churches planted. The activist can speak of people trained, mobilized, functioning. And the activist is sure that he'll get a hearing when he meets God because he's sure in his heart that God is an activist too.

IV. The Contemplative Instinct

The Agenda Is Listening

But if the activist has a plan to change some part of the world, the contemplative has something else in mind. His instinct is to meet God not in the midst of a busy project but in the quiet of his inner life: that great space of the soul where one meditates, listens, and broods on the wordless whispers of a God who meets His people in solitude and silence.

There is a rich precedent of contemplative activity in the Christ-following tradition. If the activist likes to highlight the relentless involvement of Jesus among people, the contemplative likes to point out the frequent withdrawals He made from the same people. The activist keys in on the needs of the crowds; the contemplative notes the Lord's habit of retreating into isolation so that He could commune with the Father.

The contemplative is not hostile to public corporate worship, even though he probably wishes there was more quiet than noise in the process. Nor is he neglectful in the pursuit of objectively stated truth, though he informs us that there are "doctrines" that words cannot convey. Some of the greatest worship leaders and theological minds in the Christ-following tradition are contemplatives.

Spend time with a Christ-follower whose leading instinct of the spirit is of the contemplative kind, and you will hear of his great concern that many people have all but fenced off vast areas of the soul by not paying attention to how one intersects with God through the spiritual disciplines. Do we not understand, he will challenge, that the greatest refreshments of Heaven come not in the surface water of words or feelings or even activity but in deep aquifers of the spirit, which are fed by the streams of God? This source can be tapped only by the one who shuns the din of the day and presses himself to become still. The result? The individual meets God. Then the contemplative hears; then he comes to know; then he gains guidance.

The contemplative believes that praying is a two-way conversation, and he may even say that praying is more listening than speaking. When he meets God, he does not worry about all thoughts being entirely rational or fitting together. What he wants to know is that the God who is bigger than our rational processes is impressing upon us His mysterious presence in whatever way He wants to do it. And the contemplative remarks that we will simply know when that has happened, and that's the important thing.

Some contemplatives become so serious about meeting God in the meditative way that they enter monasteries and embrace a simple, even austere, lifestyle. More than one man or woman has walked away from a lucrative career to find stillness and then become devoted to quiet, unpublicized service for others. A much smaller group of contemplatives have even chosen the permanent or temporary life of the hermit, living in enforced solitude and extended prayer.

In the organized church the Christ-follower with the contemplative instinct is most likely to ask why more people are not drawn to the prayerful life. He may appear disdainful of those who hawk great programs and yet do not seem to tap the divine energies that make programs work. He feels deeply the need to admonish us to pursue wisdom rather than knowledge, direction rather than progress. The right spiritual process impresses him more than results.

The contemplation of God within the heart and the resultant prayerful and meditative lifestyle is a strength the Asian Christ-follower has brought to the Christian community. The Asian has taught us that the wheels of time move slowly but inexorably toward what God has chosen to bring to pass. It is more important, the Asian teaches us, to be in touch with where God is moving than to expend all our energies in making that movement happen.

The contemplative Christ-follower is a distinct minority in Western Christian culture. But he or she may be increasing in number as some Christ-followers struggle with a feeling of emptiness that follows so much busyness. My sense has always been that the contemplative is a rather delicate person, somewhat like a flower—one who must be respected and protected, kind of like an endangered species.

The activist and the contemplative seem at first to be total opposites: the one moving externally, the other internally. They can easily irritate each other when they should be complementing each other. When their leading instincts are woven together, however, something very, very powerful occurs.

John the Baptizer is a marvelous example of a contemplative who added activism to his list of instincts. Forging his faith on the base of the writings of another contemplative, the Older Testament Isaiah, John spent years in the desert, pondering God's challenge of repentance to Israel. He apparently maintained strict control of physical matters such as his place of living (a cave perhaps?), his possessions (he seems to have had little more than a camel's hair coat and a leather belt, an unimaginative combination of locusts and wild honey).

One might think that the Baptizer would have been out of touch with reality when he came charging into the lives of Judean people with his thunderous pronouncements. Yet it was as if he had been filling his heart with thought and insight for years, and one day it exploded. And the introspective John, now gone public, became the talk of all Jerusalem.

When John spoke, he was right on target, and the crowds massed to hear him because they realized he was putting his finger on something they sensed was wrong but couldn't quite identify. His contemplatively gained insights cut across the grain of their activist and (perhaps) aesthetic instincts. Speaking loudly about what he'd heard in quiet, he gained their attention, and not a few believed and were prepared to see the Christ when He appeared as the Lamb of God. But the point is that it took a contemplative to get the ball rolling. Activists should never forget that!

When contemplatives and activists fail to understand one another, they run the danger of lapsing into shallowness or uselessness. Down through the centuries, some contemplatives went to the wilderness and lived in caves. Apart from the richness of some writing by a relative few of the desert fathers, it is difficult to see how this withdrawal made a contribution to the Christ-following movement. In other centuries activists formed crusading armies and decided to cleanse the world of infidels. The shallowness of such efforts did more harm than good.

But weld these two instincts together—the desire to meet God in the depths of the soul and the desire to meet Him in the streets for the purpose of sacrificial service—and you have a formidable combination of inner strength and outer resolve.

The contemplative loves to withdraw to meet God, especially because he or she is convinced beyond words that God is at heart a contemplative too.

CHAPTER EIGHT

Scholars and Peacemakers

A Thought for You, Smithy
Some smithies will insist that your faith mirror a carefully defined system. Others will insist that your faith works best in a climate of harmony and friendliness. There's merit to both perspectives. But don't favor one at the expense of the other.

The aesthete loves a litany; the experientialist loves a prophecy; the activist loves a strategy; and the contemplative loves a meditation. They bring these and many other things like them when they meet God. I call them our leading instincts of the spirit. But I wish to invite two others along in our journey of following Christ to meet the Father.

V. The Student Instinct

The Agenda Is Truth

I call the first of these two the student because truth is his great quest: truth that is conveyed in carefully crafted words and doctrines. Out of this may flow a great theology, a framework for understanding as much as possible who God is and how He acts.

If the contemplative searches out the presence of God deep within the spirit, the student believes that God is most profoundly discovered in Bible study. And that means, he says, that the Christ-follower ought to be a constant searcher of the Scripture. Thank the student for things like the Sunday school, expository sermons, and some parts of the modern Bible study movement.

The student's search for biblical truth can become a passionate pursuit, and sometimes it eventuates in loud clashes as sharp minds come up with differing conclusions about what the Scriptures say. In the Christ-following movement there are many examples of tragic rifts between well-meaning people who were willing to forfeit long-standing friendships or traditions over such a disagreement.

If the student has a blind spot, it is in a commitment to truth finding that becomes arrogant and unloving. In the worst cases, the student is capable of becoming a mean-spirited person who cares more about being right than giving preferential honor, as the Scripture puts it, to others. Garrison Keillor, looking back to his childhood student-oriented church, writes, "We had a surplus of scholars and a deficit of peace-makers."

On the other hand, the community of faith would likely disintegrate if it weren't for the student Christ-follower. History has taught us that a movement lacking a menu of well-defined beliefs and values will not last very long. So the student insists on a fervent, relentless examination of the "counsels of God" and their implications so that our faith will not be weak.

Some of the harshest words a student can level at someone are labels such as *relativist* and *heretic*. These words are used to suggest an act of deviation from orthodoxy, from a set of standard ideas about God and His revelation.

The student is suspicious when the contemplative whispers, "I sense God's presence," or the experientialist exclaims, "I feel God speaking to me," because he is more drawn to objective biblical verification. Show it to me in Scripture, he says, and then I'll agree. The student may not be impressed with the programs of the activist if he concludes that they were done for the wrong reason. More than once I have heard students dismiss an activist's successful venture by calling attention to the fact that a particular point of doctrine was not adequately observed or that the people who participated did not agree on the same set of truths.

Most students see biblical themes as pieces of a great jigsaw puzzle, all fitting perfectly and creating a marvelous picture of God's activity in history. If two pieces appear to clash, there has got to be a reason, the student says, and it is usually because the interpreter has employed faulty methods to define the truth.

The student believes that God is met and heard most powerfully by people who have put the truth first and foremost in their spiritual quest. Those who believe rightly hear God best, thus the great premium put upon teaching truth. And the teachers who can break these truths down into comprehensible and manageable segments become the most popular.

Again, if it were not for the student with his stress on pursuing the truth about the God of the Bible, our faith would quickly sink into a disastrous relativism. We have therefore to thank the student for our creeds and for our historical defenses of the faith against its antagonists. We have the student to recognize when it comes to formulating our doctrines and being able to put our faith into practical definition. It is the student who challenges us to the development of a theological thought process, and that's not all bad.

St. Paul was doubtless a student type. He had been trained that way long before he converted to following Christ. He was certainly an activist who wanted to see the church expand, but he evidently felt it was more important for the truth to be told from synagogue to synagogue and among all peoples who would listen. He was a tireless teacher who appears to have engaged in the teaching of the truth until his dying gasp.

Although Paul gives evidence of a wonderful balance of virtually all the leading instincts of the spirit that I have described, "studenting" is the predominant one. He shows us the best side of the student, and in his humanness, he reveals a hint of the worst side.

His best side? His unvarnished love for the revealed verities of God. Many of us have responded to his vigorous plea that the young men and women of the faith become disciplined students of the Scripture. His relentless effort to formulate answers to the questions new believers might ask and to challenge those who tried to influence the church to deviant doctrines has provided a remarkable theological heritage.

And the dark side? The apostle was probably too opinionated at times. So self-assured was he that he risked losing a partnership with his old friend, Barnabas, in a dispute about John Mark's value as a working companion. How he could have risked a friendship on an opinion is frankly confusing to me. But then I've seen others do the same thing.

Then there was the time Paul confronted his fellow apostle, Peter, on a matter of practical faith and did it in front of all of his friends. The modern student Christ-follower doesn't hesitate to affirm the correctness of Paul's action. But some like myself would have at least thought to take Peter on a walk and ask him some gentle questions to get to the point. That way he wouldn't have been humiliated.

Lest I be unfair in my view of Paul, he was not always so hard-nosed. I appreciate his spirit, for example, in tolerating the Roman Christ-followers who preached the gospel hoping to wrest leadership away from him while he was in prison. He mourned their motives, he said, but he was nevertheless more than glad that the story of Jesus was being told on the streets of Rome—whatever the reason. But I must tell you, I still wouldn't want to ever get in his way when his mind went to work on a thought. That man was the consummate student!

The student is never more at home than when turning to the Bible and discovering what he or she perceives to be a new truth or insight that has never been identified before. In fact the student has this view of the Heavenlies: it all will be one eternal Bible study with God as discussion leader. For the student thinks he can point to a text of Scripture proving beyond reasonable doubt that God is a student too.

The counterpoint to the student is what I call the relationalist.

VI. The Relational Instinct

The Agenda Is Love

If the student speaks of a love for truth, the relationalist speaks of a love for people. Obviously these loves are not mutually exclusive. But since we're talking about leading instincts of the spirit—those ways in which a person is most likely to want to meet and please God—it almost sounds like that.

The relationalist is convinced that God is most present and intimate when people experience an unusual bonding together for fellowship or worship or mutual support. It tickles him (and horrifies the contemplative) to think that when we follow Christ into the presence of the Father, we might go in groups and have a marvelous time . . . together.

The relationalist swims in people values. He wants to bring Christ-followers together to serve and enjoy one another. He is heartbroken if there is conflict; and he is dispirited if people do not open their lives in honesty and candor. Conversely, he is exhilarated if he senses that people are breaking down barriers of misunderstanding that have normally divided them. When this happens, he believes he sees God at work, and he feels that he has met Him most intimately in that hour.

Relationalists love meetings. Not the kind held in rooms where chairs are placed in long straight lines facing a podium. That means a lecture. But the kind where the chairs are placed in small circles; that implies intimacy. Relationalists covet times when people are free to tell their personal stories. They fairly salivate when they see men and women who have had great conflicts come to a point of reconciliation.

If students love Paul, relationalists love Barnabas, Paul's first partner. It's interesting that these two got along together as long as they did. I suspect the major share of the credit goes to Barnabas.

The relationalist isn't surprised that Barnabas finally got fed up with Paul and separated from him over the John Mark matter. After all, it was Barnabas who had once taken Paul (when he was a relatively new Christ-follower) and introduced him to a group of Jerusalem church leaders who found it difficult to lower their guard against him. It was Barnabas who had later visited a band of new Christ-followers in the town of Antioch and realized that they needed teaching and who then got Paul there to help make it happen. And it was Barnabas who had taken John Mark under his wing and mentored him. So when Paul the student rejected John Mark because of a previous failure, Barnabas the relationalist became adamant and dissolved the partnership. Every time you notice Barnabas, he seems to be looking out for the welfare and relationships of people. Today's relationalist loves that man.

Relationalists have their own view of Jesus. They can accept the perspective of the activists, namely, that Jesus was a pretty busy Man dealing with large crowds and great opportunities. And they can appreciate the contemplatives' observation that Jesus often disengaged for times of silence. *But* relationalists exclaim, "Have you noted how people-conscious He was; how He always had time for the needy individual? Have you pondered His command to the Twelve, that they should love one another as a sign of authentic discipleship?"

People were Jesus' business: the lost, the despised, the wounded, the unappreciated. Wherever He went, He gave Himself to people and built up their sense of hope and value and wholeness. He introduced them to God and then to one another.

And that's what the relationalist loves to do best. When it is happening, he has no doubt: God is present, and the Heavens are rejoicing. And why all this rejoicing? The relationalist will tell you if you ask. He is positive that when all is said and done, when we have had time to explore the being of God to greater depths as He reveals Himself, we'll find out that God is a relationalist too.

The Conclusion of the Matter

Jesus Christ possessed every one of these six leading instincts of the spirit. He was a contemplative; but He was also an activist. Jesus was a relationalist; but He was also a student. And Jesus was an experientialist; but, yes, he was also an aesthete. He mixed all six, perfectly, in a balanced way.

My sense is that most of us will possess a natural inclination for two or three of the six, a curiosity about one or two more, but we will struggle to even believe that what's left over has any value at all.

In the forging of a real-world faith, we must remember that one of the first places Christ leads us is into the presence of His Father. How will we know that we are there, and what will we do in His presence? Most likely, the answers to these questions will come as we identify and appreciate the ways in which we are most comfortable in being in His presence.

We identify the leading instincts by simply observing what is most natural for us to do in expressing ourselves to God and in receiving His word to us. But when we have discovered what is most natural, it is important to explore the other four or five. Maturity in faith comes as we become conversant in all six languages of worship as Christ was.

I began this set of descriptions by telling you of an upsetting experience I had on an airplane after I had been greatly touched by a sense of God's presence. What had gripped me that day had been drawn into my inner being through the instincts of the experientialist (I had felt deep feelings of conviction), the relationalist (I felt that others were strongly involved as I was), and the contemplative (I sensed the mighty hand of God at work).

But I permitted two "students" to go to work on me. Good men, those students. But that day they needed more sensitivity, and I needed more courage. Their objectivity was a bucket of cold water thrown on my passion. We all probably had something to learn that day, and we missed it. And that may be how many opportunities to meet God as we follow Christ into the Heavenlies are missed.

CHAPTER NINE

God Is Not Like
George Burns

A Thought for You, Smithy
Forging a faith may at times seem an effort that
asks too much of you, Smithy. You will wish to
turn away and get on with things that appear to
be simpler and more profitable. Don't! Do the
hard thing. Choose to joyfully work in the pres-
ence of a Master who is greater than yourself.

C. S. Lewis writes of "a schoolboy who was asked what he thought
God was like. [The boy] replied that, as far as he could make out,
God was 'the sort of person who is always snooping around to see if
anyone is enjoying himself and then trying to stop it.''

That's an intriguing view of God and His activities. Is it unique?
Probably not. You can find insufficient theologies almost anyplace if
you ask the right questions and keep your ear to the ground.

Walking into a local coffee shop at 5:45 in the morning, I see a small
knot of men I know who usually start their day there. A conversation
with one of them develops off to one side as we drink our coffee and
eat English muffins. He mentions something about his church, and it
causes me to ask further about his religious life since I hadn't known
he had one. He is quite straightforward about the fact that he is in
church every Sunday, and we drift into a rather interesting conversation about God in our lives.

"Look," I say at one point, lowering my voice to emphasize that
this topic is strictly between us, "so you've been going to church for
years. Why? What keeps you going back week after week?"

He ponders the question for a moment, and I have the feeling that he's making up his mind whether he will tell me what he thinks I want to hear or what really drives him in that section of his life.

He apparently opts for the latter and adopts something of a tough style in the way he begins to talk as if he's got to underscore his masculinity.

"You really want to now why? I'll tell you why." Before he continues, he actually looks from side to side as if he wants to assure himself that he's not being overheard. "I've been going to church all my life. I've got a good wife and two grown daughters who are happily married and giving me grandchildren. They all love me. My job is going well; I've only got about eight more years to retirement. I'm healthy. Nothing's gone wrong; you know what I mean? Now why fool around with a good thing? I mean, don't change nothing when you like things the way they are. So that's why I go to church." And then he speaks very slowly and very confidentially, "Shoot, you know; I don't want God mad at me now. You see what I mean?"

I guess I've never forgotten that conversation (and I've written of it before) because my breakfast-mate's conclusions were expressed with such utter simplicity and frankness. I saw no indication that he was out to fool with me. He meant what he said: he perceived he had struck a bargain with God. He'd do his part on Sunday, God's day, if God did His part during the weekdays, my friend's days.

Both the man in the coffee shop and the boy in C. S. Lewis's story possessed a theology; it amounted to a perception of God and the kind of things He might or might not do when He intersects with human life. The child saw God as a mean old man. My breakfast-mate saw God as a deal maker; in this case, the terms were a man's religious activity in exchange for a divine pledge not to vandalize a good life. Both theologies are unfortunate; both are quite similar; and both are easy to see through. But both are not unusual. They are the stuff of which defective faith is made.

No faith is ready for action in the real world if it is not grounded in a better understanding of God than this. But perhaps it would be beneficial if we became unusually candid with ourselves and asked if our personal views of God—who He is and what He does—are substantially better. Who is my God? Has it occurred to me that time regularly taken to resolve that question could be some of the most useful time in the schedule? For many years, in my case, it did not. I love the beginning of a book called *How to Keep God Alive From 9 to 5* by New York publisher John Chervokas, who writes,

This book makes three assumptions. Those assumptions are:
1. There is a God.
2. He is not George Burns.
3. God works where we work.

Chervokas seems to have an outlook similar to mine. What you know and think of God—realize it or not—will be an indispensable element in the forging of a real-world faith.

It took me more than thirty years of living before I began to take seriously this question of who God was. That is not to say I hadn't chosen to become a Christ-follower long before. And I had already engaged in graduate work at seminary, regular preaching and pastoring in a church, and my first attempts at writing. I had passed the ordination exams, and I had introduced more than one person to an experience of Christ-following.

But was I growing in my awareness of who God was? Was I thinking critically of how I should act in His presence? Was I, in fact, coming to terms at all with the idea that Christ-following meant learning how to live in humility and devotion to the Everlasting Father, the Creator of the world?

I knew the formal theological constructions of both the conservative and the liberal views of God, and I knew the traditional terms and phrases easily batted about in Christ-following circles like a tennis ball over a net. But I had limited experience when it came to being utterly captured, consumed by the glory and majesty of our God. Strange as it may seem, I had not yet learned to fear Him (as the Bible speaks of fearing God); I had not learned how to properly reverence Him; and I had not grown curious enough to pursue a growing knowledge of the mysteries of His personhood.

If the God of my childhood was an old man who lived at the top of a steel ladder and engaged in trivial pursuits, the God of my young adulthood was a distant chairman-of-the-board type who was there (and somehow very important) but not there enough to play a significant role in my routines of life. I was comfortable in a perceived relationship with Jesus the Son, and I was anxious to draw from what I learned was power from the Holy Spirit. But the "chairman of the board" remained an illusive "player" in my world.

If I did not know for sure that I was not alone in this theology, which was as innocuous as the theology of the boy and of the man with whom this chapter began, I would be greatly embarrassed to admit my shallowness. In his landmark book, *Knowing God,* J. I. Packer was quite candid when he wrote,

> We need frankly to face ourselves at this point. We are, perhaps, orthodox evangelicals. We can state the gospel clearly, and can smell unsound doctrine a mile away. If anyone asks us how men may know God, we can at once produce the right formulae—that we come to know God through Jesus Christ the Lord, in virtue of His cross and mediation, on the basis of His word of promise, by the power of the Holy Spirit, via a personal exercise of faith. Yet the gaiety, goodness, and unfetteredness of spirit which are the marks of those who have known God are rare among us—rarer perhaps than they are in some other Christian circles where, by comparison, evangelical truth is less clearly and fully known. Here, too, it would seem that the last may prove to be first, and the first last. A little knowledge of God is worth more than a great deal of knowledge about Him.

Those words were a tremendous rebuke. Perhaps I was being a bit hard on myself, but as far as I could see, Packer was describing me as one of those in need of "gaiety, goodness, and unfetteredness of spirit." If there was any particular experience that brought the issue of meeting and reverencing God as He really is into focus for me, it was one morning when I was crossing the battlegreen in Lexington, Massachusetts. There, more than two hundred years ago, the minutemen from local towns made a brave stand against a much larger British redcoat contingent marching from Boston to Concord. Today at the Lexington common are several monuments erected in memory to the men who fought there. Some of them were placed there by the first generation of Americans who had lived through those testy days.

Read the inscriptions on those monuments, and you realize how much those people hated the king of England and everything attached to royalty. That morning, as I read some of those volatile words pertaining to the "tyrant," the "oppressor" from across the sea, I was suddenly struck with the realization that our entire American culture has been permeated with an antiroyal bias.

The anger and the resistance from those earliest days remain strangely with us in the United States and fuel the tradition that there could never be a royal personage ruling sovereignly over us. A dictator someday? Always a possibility when the privileges of freedom are squandered. But a king? Never! The good news is that we enjoy a flourishing democratic tradition. The bad news is that it has cost us our understanding of reverence and respect for majesty. Thus our loss of capacity to exercise a general sense of awe and wonder about much of anything except beautiful sunsets, outstanding athletic achievements, and new electronic gadgets.

I believe this is a key reason why many of us in America have such an inferior view of God. We have never learned to enter with reverence into the presence of royalty: earthly *or* Heavenly. The president of the United States is as close as we come to someone highly revered, but even he serves only at the pleasure of the people. As soon as we (or the Constitution with its two-term limit) are through with the president, we elect someone else. We respect the office far more than the person.

Our lack of experience in reverence has to affect our ability to worship God. Most of us can handle the notion of walking with Jesus; few of us can manage the thought of falling prostrate on our faces before the King of all creation.

This insight at the Lexington battlegreen was augmented a while later when I was the guest of friends in London for the parade of the queen's Horse Guards in annual commemoration of her birthday. In England the event is known as the Trooping of the Color. It was an awesome moment when the queen entered the parade grounds sitting astride a coal black horse to review her guards. We all stood, and I could feel the powerful sense of esteem and affection that the English about me felt for their queen. Not a person moved; there was no sound to be heard except the horses' hoofbeats. I think every eye was fixed upon the queen. One hardly dared breathe.

The loop of insight that began at the Lexington battlegreen was suddenly closed for me. *So this,* I thought, *is what it is like to give reverence to majesty. This is something of what it might be like to stand with the company of the saints before the throne of God in silence or in loud praise and to worship the Lord of Heaven and earth.* For me, it was important to have a sample experience, even if it could not compare to the worship of the saints before the divine throne on the (forgive my triteness) Heavenly parade grounds. At least now I had a vision of high reverence that I had never gained in a church or in any other meeting where it was rumored that God was present.

The question arises, then, in this twentieth-century period of time

when increasing numbers of people in Western civilization care little
about any god or, if they do, know little about how to meet him:

> How can we who are Christ-followers formulate an enlarging view
> of our Creator and our proper posture before Him that will guide
> the forging of a real-world faith?

Perhaps the only way to address such a question is to take a hard
look at people of the Bible who had some remarkable experiences that
brought them close to the majestic presence of Heavenly royalty.

I confess without hesitation the difficulty in writing on this matter
of knowing and understanding God. It is a formidable topic usually left
to the scholar who packages it all in a vocabulary often beyond the
grasp or interest of people of the street. I have sat for hours at the
keyboard of my computer trying to put together words that satisfy
what I feel, and I come up with virtually nothing worthy of the subject.
I have desperately wanted to quit, to call my publisher and tell him I
have tackled a subject too large for me. I want him to release me from
my commitment to finish this book because I cannot come to terms
with this awesome task. And then just as I reach for the switch to turn
off the machine, something within me says, "Stop! God has not made
Himself a subject to be handled only by the theologian. He is a God for
every person who believes." His glory and honor are not to be observed only by the trained academician; it is a matter revealed to plain
people such as the shepherds in the countryside the night Jesus was
born or the aged people who waited for news of Messiah's birth. The
disclosure of His glory came to the simple people of the street. And
they were innocent enough to receive it for what it was worth. They
fell to their knees and worshiped. Somehow, they instinctively understood how to act in the presence of a Holy God.

I am quite comfortable with shepherds and peasants. If they are
the kinds of folks God most easily deals with when it comes to the
subject of majesty, I'll press on and assume I'm writing to them.

Whether it is a boy with a view of a mean God, a laboring man with
a bargaining view of God, or a host of us with a benign view of God,
the problem will always be the same: one's faith will be built on an
inadequate foundation. Weak God; weak faith. Weak faith; harassment
in the real world.

CHAPTER TEN

God Was in Control

A Thought for You, Smithy
Smithy, when you're forging a faith, don't get trapped by small things so that the big view is obscured. Remember:
Who called you to this task
Why you started swinging your hammer
What the finished product is going to look like
Your pursuit is a noble thing. Seize it with enthusiasm and expectation.

In the New Testament book of Revelation, the author John (not to be forgotten as a retired fisherman) tells the reader of a visionary experience in the place called Heaven. He had been invited, he said, to climb the "steel ladder" (my words) and peer through the trapdoor to see what was going on.

Each time I read of his invitation to look in on Heaven, I think of the day I climbed the steel ladder in my church and looked out a cluttered balcony. Hardly Heaven! My experience was deflating; John's was inflating. My imagination was stripped of its illusions; his was enlarged by things so magnificent that he was left swimming in superlatives and imagery.

Why was John selected to be a guest for this overwhelming experience? I believe it had something to do with the fact that he was to be a historian of the future. His apostolic task was to convey to the Christ-followers of succeeding generations an overarching scheme of the times. He was to warn us of the sinister conspiracies of evil. He was to write of judgments and blessings, suffering and crowning, defeats and victories among the nations. And most important, he was to affirm for us that Christ our Savior would someday return and assert kingly control over all elements of creation, whether they resisted or not. John was mandated to write about an immense view of time. It was designed to generate hope, stamina of the spirit, and confidence in God: things real-world faith badly needs.

But how could John be brazen enough to convey this enormous vision of history to paper if he was not convinced that it was an authentic theme originated in the heart of the God of history? How could he form a view of the real world unless he was sure? He couldn't! And thus his sense of certainty about these things was formed through an invitation to Heavenly worship where he might see as best he could the glory of God and how the saints on the Heavenly parade ground gave homage to the Eternal Sovereign.

John was not the first to meet God in this way. Abraham's real-world faith was forged in encounters with God at altars of sacrifice. He was never the same again. Moses begged God for a view of His glory on the mountaintop and finally got a glimpse of it. It kept him going when most of us, without such a vision, would have resigned, effective immediately, from running the Hebrew wilderness tour.

Isaiah saw the glory of God in some sort of temple while Paul saw it on the road to Damascus. Mary, the mother of the Lord, came into contact with it through an angel. The list goes on of people who in varying ways met God and, as a result, developed a real-world faith that serves as a model for us all.

Back to John. His vision is the most detailed and the most useful of all because he describes what amounts to a Heavenly worship service with a liturgy that is easy to follow and quite instructive. John helped me to understand two things: first, something about how great God is and how He wants to be seen, and second, how people who care about God respond to Him. That's useful information for someone who wishes to walk in connection with God in a real world.

I lead a group of people in worship in the heart of New York City every Sunday, and John has been a great source of encouragement as to how a congregation might walk through an encounter with God when many have been beaten up by the system all week long and have arrived in the sanctuary on the Lord's Day full of fatigue and confusion. Knowing how the Heavenly family chose to meet God and worship Him, I want to make sure that our congregation does as much of the same thing as possible.

What John seems to have witnessed specifically was something like a Heavenly hymn-sing. The content of the songs he records is significant because it appears to form an outline for the themes one might want to keep in mind in the forging of real-world faith on a daily basis.

For example, I hear the order of the Heavenly songs something like this. First, a song about the ATTRIBUTES of God: who He is. Second, a song about the MIGHTY ACTS of God: things He has done. Third, a song about the ACCEPTING WORK of God: the particular way in which He has connected with broken people via the Cross. And finally, a song of ASCRIPTION: thanksgiving and praise about the worth of God, if indeed one could dare to think of computing it.

Is this theology? Of course! Is it practical? I mean, does it really make any difference in the real world whether or not these things are known and appreciated? My mind scans the list of some people I've encountered this week. The woman who is managing bond accounts at Fifth Avenue and Forty-fourth Street in New York. The folks I've been with who work in arbitrage on Sixth and Fifty-second. Or the dancers, the actors, and the musicians who work on Broadway and were in church on Sunday. The retired woman over on the West Side who lives alone and fears her health is failing her, the man without a home who lives in a shelter near Riverside Drive, or a bunch of others who are in advertising, communications, the UN, and small businesses. And what of those I know who have AIDS, who are struggling with addictions, or who have stumbled into failure? Can it make a difference for them?

I can tell you what difference John's vision makes for me. I have used these words—*attributes, acts, acceptance, ascription*—to form an outline for my personal meditations in my quiet moments or in my hassled moments throughout the day.

Living in New York provides one an opportunity for much walking. And as I walk the streets and read the signs on the magnificent buildings that speak of world-famous company names, I am tempted to reorient the base of my faith to something visible and immediate. And then I remember the great attributes of God and pray, *IBM has a great name, but You, O Lord, have a name above all names, a name echoed continuously in the Heavens.* IBM's name will one day be merely a footnote in history (stockholders should be forewarned), but the name of God will live forever. I would think my friends in the corporate world would profit from keeping the attributes of God in mind when they are tempted to think they are running the world.

At a lunchtime meeting someone points out a world-renowned

personality across the room. I've seen his picture on magazine covers; he consults with the president regularly. He makes things happen. I am tempted to an interior adulation that is absurd. And then I remember the mighty acts of God and pray, *But You, O Lord, have done the truly great things that cannot be defeated or reversed. He may orchestrate a leveraged buy-out that will earn the investors billions, but You have orchestrated the creation of Heaven and earth with nothing but a word, and the whole thing keeps going from hour to hour simply because You keep on saying so.* I would think the folks in financial matters would want to regularly review the mighty acts of God and remember that there are more important things than the slide of an eighth point on a particular stock.

The phone rings one morning, and I am invited to give a talk at what I consider to be a significant function. And when I end the conversation, I am aware of something growing within me that makes me feel important and very valuable. But this is a dangerous and an illusory feeling, and I am quickly reminded of a recent time in my life when very few saw much value in me. Except God! And He as Creator and Redeemer loved me and valued me as much in my totally broken moment as He might on another day when life seems a bit more put together. The invitation hasn't added one cent of value to me that God hasn't put there first by accepting me. I would hope that some of those who perceive themselves to be powerless because they're aging, broken, or very sick would understand that they are as valuable to the Lord as anyone who would gain the attention of the world.

I am sleepless in the middle of the night. Perhaps I went to bed thinking about too many things, and my mind will not turn off and open the way to rest. The internal computer runs on and on processing this book manuscript, problems, programs, and people with whom I am involved. And I cannot seem to bring the mind to control until I concentrate on ascriptions, praises to God. I press my mind to ponder the worth of God: *All these things seem so important; but You, O Lord, are the sum total of everything. It is all Yours; it comes from You and returns to You. I am Your child. While I seek to sleep, You never stop watching over creation. Of what conceivable use is my worry or my fear?*

Slowly, things within come to rest. And before long the Spirit of the Lord gives rest to a formerly restless night.

These meditations are John's gifts. The size of things, the importance of things, the value of things, the majesty of things—these are contributing elements to real-world faith. And I got them from John who seems to have learned them at a Heavenly worship service when he heard the angels and the saints sing. Look over his shoulder with me.

The Attributes

The first thing John heard was the opening hymn of the Heavenly family, which focused on some of God's attributes. They were statements about who God is.

> Holy, holy, holy is the Lord God Almighty, who was, and is, and is to come (Rev. 4:8).

Attributes are those qualities about the person of God that He has chosen to reveal to us. There are probably many more attributes He hasn't chosen to reveal yet. In this brief accolade sung to God by the Heavenly family, at least four attributes were acknowledged: His holiness (and that emphasized three times, which suggests an infinitude of holiness), His lordship (or His sovereignty), His power (the Almighty), and His everlasting nature (He was, is, and is to come).

The Christ-followers of Heaven teach you and me a fundamental lesson as they sing of attributes first. They tell us that one of the very first things an individual does whenever he enters into God's presence is to celebrate the things known about God. The attributes the Heavenly family chose in this case stretch the inner spirit because they speak about dimensions of immensity far exceeding our human understanding.

We are challenged to ponder a God who is infinitely holy or pure and totally untouched by the pollution of evil. We are invited to think about a God who is sovereign Lord, whose word alone is law for the universe. He is all-powerful.

Then there is the attribute concerning God's everlasting nature. The matter sends the mind spinning, for we have been taught from the beginning that everything is subject to a cycle of birth and death. But God is not! And that truth alone should cause the worshiper to kneel in awe and respect.

The Mighty Acts

Soon after, the Heavenly family begins a second section of worship before the Lord. Now the song centers on God's mighty acts. What has God done?

You are worthy, our Lord and God, to receive glory and honor and power, for you created all things, and by your will they were created and have their being (Rev. 4:11).

This God is not a gigantic Buddha, an animistic worship object, or a amorphous gas hanging somewhere out in space. He has done and is doing certain things that deserve our attention.

The attention given by the Heavenly family now has to do with recognizing what God has done. He created all things, *and* by the constant exertion of the energy of His will, all things keep on existing. Should God change His mind about keeping things going, a simple consequence would follow: everything would suddenly cease to exist just as a balloon would collapse if the one blowing it up were to stop filling it with air.

If God chose, Wall Street would cease to exist; the buildings of Westminster and the marvelous clock tower we call Big Ben would disappear; the combined armies of NATO and the Warsaw Pact would no longer be armies.

This company of worshipers John has joined declares something that we do not think about enough: the Lord God of Jesus Christ made everything, owns everything, and keeps everything going. One thought from His mind, and all these things that we hold onto so tightly will disappear. Our wealth, our health, our potential—all belong to Him and exist only at His pleasure. And that is what this hymn sung in the Heavenlies is all about.

This stunning reality (not new; just not thought about enough) is sure to reorient the thinking of the Christ-follower. Next to this kind of God whose attributes and acts are stupendous, one's boss, one's company, and one's city seem quite puny.

This in part is why Jesus was fearless as the incarnate Savior when He stood before Pontius Pilate. Pilate was upset that Jesus paid him such little respect.

"Don't you realize I have power either to free you or to crucify you?" the Roman asked his prisoner (John 19:10).

"You would have no power over me if it were not given to you from above," Jesus answered.

What was happening? Jesus was simply operating on a practical knowledge of both the attributes and the acts of His Father. Just as Daniel had been fearless for the very same reason, Jesus was thinking in total independence of the human system. Why? Because He knew who was really in charge, and nothing was going to occur that was not in accord with the purposes of His Father. Pilate's cross may have been in Jesus' immediate future but only because it was permitted in the sovereign design of a greater God.

Centuries before Jesus stood before Pilate, the servant of Elisha (protégé of Elijah) stepped out of their home one morning and froze. Surrounding the town was an army of horses and chariots; and its mission was to find Elisha and kidnap him.

The most intelligent thing the servant could think to say to his master was, "Oh, my lord [meaning Elisha, not God], what shall we do?" (2 Kings 6:15).

"Don't be afraid," Elisha responded. "Those who are with us are more than those who are with them."

That's an interesting assessment when all one can see with his eyes is an intimidating war machine and no defenses. Most of us have had an experience in life when the field of vision seemed to contain all enemies and no friends. So it seemed to Elisha's servant.

Elisha prayed, "O LORD [now it's God], open his eyes so he may see."

The Bible records, "Then the LORD opened the servant's eyes, and he looked and saw the hills full of horses and chariots of fire all around Elisha."

The Bible is full of stories like this. And every time it is the same. A power clash occurs. And what seems at first to be a threatening situation turns out to be the opposite because the God of Heaven is greater in attribute and action than the entities of power on earth.

This is real-world faith in action in the midst of a turbulent system. Jesus stands like a rock, and we are left to watch Pilate become the one in actual bondage. Elisha stands tall, and we get to watch his confident adversaries end up the fools. There's a kind of humor in all of this when you think about it.

In her book *Life and Death in Shanghai* Nien Cheng writes of her experiences in a prison during the Chinese cultural revolution. In chapter after chapter she describes the brutality of her captors as they attempted to break her will and force from her a confession of conspiracy against the government of the People's Republic of China. But she would not break, and she constantly affirmed her innocence. Mrs. Cheng was a widow, and she was separated from her only daughter (much later, Mrs. Cheng would learn she was dead). Apart from her faith—which was obviously of the real-world kind—she had nothing as a resource upon which to rely.

At a key moment in her incarceration, Mrs. Cheng writes, she saw a tiny spider ("the creature was no bigger than a good sized pea") crawling up the side of the cell window. When it had climbed to the top, it began the intricate process of spinning a web: "It swung out and descended on a thin silken thread spun from one end of its body. With a leap and swing, it secured the end of the thread to another bar." This process, Mrs. Cheng recalls, happened over and over again until there was a frame upon which to build a web: "There was no hesitation, no mistake, and no haste. It knew its job and was carrying it out with confidence." When the spider's task was complete, it "went to its center and settled there."

Nien Cheng suggests what this meant to her:

I had just watched an architectural feat by an extremely skilled artist, and my mind was full of questions. Who had taught the spider how to make a web? Could it really have acquired the skill through evolution, or did God create the spider and endow it with the ability to make a web so that it could catch food and perpetuate its species?

And then she concludes:

For the moment I knew I had just witnessed something that was extraordinarily beautiful and uplifting. Whether God had made the spider or not, I thanked Him for what I had just seen. A miracle of life had been shown me. *It helped me to see that God was in control. Mao Zedong and his Revolutionaries seemed much less menacing. I felt a renewal of hope and confidence.* (Emphasis mine)

This is theology in a prison cell: theology of a real-world kind that converts into something, in this case "hope and confidence." Interestingly enough, I learned long after I read *Life and Death in Shanghai* that when the book was published in various European languages, publishers removed this passage about the spider. I find this remarkable. In their desire to remove all theological references in Nien Cheng's account of her terrible ordeal, they were not perceptive enough to realize they were editing out the core thing—her real-world faith—that made her capable of survival. The thing they chose to delete was the key to what made it possible for them to ever have a book to sell.

Whether it is the performance of a tiny spider in a Chinese prison cell or the force of a powerful choir singing in the Heavenlies, the message is the same: our God is great, and His acts are great. Nothing in the world can thwart this God of ours; nothing can prevail against Him.

This is the big view, and it was celebrated that day in Heaven when John peeked through the door. He saw other things of course, but those are for another chapter.

CHAPTER ELEVEN

Jailhouse Songs

A Thought for You, Smithy
No forging of faith is without failure. Some things can be corrected; some things cannot. Remember, you are working for a Master of grace, and even the mistakes will be turned into something useful. In this workplace there are no discards.

My imagination runs wild with the imagery of John climbing into Heaven from his steel ladder. I see him gain more confidence as the timeless moments pass and he listens to the choirs sing about the attributes and acts of God. Does he step closer and closer so that he can see more?

The Theme of Acceptance

A third event in the worship of the Heavenly company is about to begin. John writes that he saw a scroll (an ancient book) sealed with seven seals. Interpreters have wondered for centuries what that scroll contained. The names of all of God's people? The scheme of history as God has planned it from before the creation of the earth? Whatever the content, the remarkable thing is that no one, John says, had the credentials to break the seals and investigate the contents.

This caused John to react emotionally. "I wept and wept," he wrote, "because no one was found who was worthy to open the scroll" (Rev. 5:4).

But John wept only because he had not seen a principal figure in the drama apparently off to one side. It was a lamb (also called, para-doxically, the lion of the tribe of Judah) that, though alive, had the marks of being freshly slaughtered. The images grew more complex. It was the Lamb of God whom we know to be Christ Himself.

And suddenly John was aware. This was the solitary One who had power to open the scroll. Again, the choir burst into praise, this time singing to the Lamb:

> You are worthy to take the scroll and to open its seals, because you were slain, and with your blood you purchased men for God from every tribe and language and people and nation. You have made them to be a kingdom and priests to serve our God, and they will reign on the earth (Rev. 5:9–10).

The third great theme that the Heavenly choir sought to highlight has to do with acceptance through redemption or reclamation. At issue here are the Cross and what the Lamb of God accomplished as the once-and-for-all sacrifice for the sins of humanity.

In just a few sentences of hymnody the choir raised all sorts of remarkable truths about God's purposes: the act of atonement, the multicultural and multinational character of the family of God, the call for the saints to be priests and servants in a kingdom that will reign forever.

If there is a key issue here, it is Christ making all things new in the lives of broken people from every age. Christ doing what seems impossible for anyone else to do—bring new life to the living dead.

I walk New York's streets and see a cross section of the people this hymn features. *The Lamb was slaughtered on behalf of the people I see on those streets.* Now a practical aspect of a developing real-world faith suddenly falls into place. How shall people be treated here in this city? Answer: as the Lamb treated them in the giving of His life for them. I must treat all people with respect (poor or rich), with value, with the intention in mind of serving whenever possible to let the work of the Lamb be seen in my life.

I begin to think back on the times I sat in churches I entered with a broken heart. In such a time, what was I seeking? It's a reminder that I, although a sinner, was accepted by God through the gracious act of the Lamb upon the cross. When a person is overwhelmed by guilt and confused about how things in life have suddenly turned so sour, he or she needs those who will affirm that the grace of God is available to everyone. That person has to hear it tenderly spoken in a prayer, confidently sung in a song, meaningfully declared and applied in a sermon.

Then hope grows again. How many broken people walk into religious convocations every week and hear none of the themes sung in John's vision?

What is life without the act of the Lamb? Each day as a woman or man goes through the tasks of making a living, raising a family, or developing friendships, a thousand and one choices are made. Who can make them all correctly? Who can go through a day without inadvertently offending someone? Who can be sure that the inner being is not marked with substandard motives and desires that produce agendas so hidden we are not fully aware of what we are doing? Does anyone really think that there are only a few simple sins easily codified and defined? Or have we all come to gloomily realize that evil permeates the human condition and that were it not for the Lamb who becomes our friend and makes it possible for us to receive the acceptance of God, we would all be doomed?

We go then into the real world knowing that our acceptance by the Creator is not based on achievement or human acclimation. It is based on the love of the Lamb, and we stand equal with everyone in the world who has drawn upon His gift of the cross.

Sing to the freshly slaughtered Lamb, who is raised up as the lion. Sing in your heart, loud and long, in the churches, on the streets, in the bed at night, in the quiet of the office, in the car, in the lunchroom. It is the Lamb who brings sanity to life and makes us brave enough to rise from one failure after another to try again. It is the Lamb who brings humility when we have done our best and won handily. Sing to the Lamb. He is at the base of our real-world faith.

I began to understand that the Heavenly service John the Apostle visited is not other-world oriented. If it is designed to gratify the Lord to whom it is directed, it is also designed to be my personal fortification. It gives me a framework of reality from which to operate as I reenter the streets. Do I dare enter the real world each day without a worship experience reflecting what John described?

The Ascription

As the service of worship in Heaven to which John had been invited reached its conclusion, the choir sang something like a benediction:

To him who sits on the throne and to the Lamb be praise and honor and glory and power, for ever and ever! (Rev. 5:13).

More than one reader who has been kind enough to get this book will be tempted to bypass these pages about worshiping God. The individuals who deal every day with the stuff of the real world will see little or no point to worrying about what is going on in Heaven. Theirs will be a concern for holding up under the stress of modern life, keeping faithful to a spouse, figuring out how to keep children away from drugs, how to be reasonably kind to the person who has to be fired (or the one firing you), and what to do about the problem of money (either earned or coveted). Real things of that nature.

But this decision to ignore the activities of Heaven that John witnessed renders what faith one has to be weak and insufficient when it comes to addressing those kinds of issues. These immediate matters *find their scale of size only when one has FIRST learned what it means to understand and know God.* Only then is one prepared to take the next step onward in forging a real-world faith.

As the Heavenly gathering wound down, it seems to have wished to ascribe to God several great values: praise, honor, glory, and power. I believe that it was quite important for John to climb back down through the "trapdoor" with these words echoing in his mind. Implanted within him, they would refresh him concerning God's grandeur as he wrote the Revelation and traced the course of future history. There was no way he could write what he did if he was not absolutely convinced that the God of Heaven was the Lord of history.

Such an ascription of value to God needs to be implanted within the Christ-follower also. An ascription that can serve as a reminder over and over again as to who is in charge of the universe when I am tempted to doubt.

I sit at the bedside of a person with an advanced case of AIDS. He is a Christ-follower. And now he fights for his life. He has lost control of everything we take for granted. His environment is controlled by medical personnel. His body has lost control to the disease. His mind fights for control, for some inner forces would like to create despair and hopelessness.

After we have visited about personal matters, I suggest that we have a Bible reading, and he nods in agreement. I decide that he needs to hear some ascriptions to God that will bolster confidence. I turn immediately to Psalm 91 and begin to read slowly so that every word will sink in to a tired mind and heart:

Whoever goes to the Lord for safety,
whoever remains under the
    protection of the Almighty,
can say to him,
    "You are my defender and protector.
    You are my God; in you I trust." . . .
God says, "I will save those who love me
    and will protect those who know me as Lord.
When they call to me, I will answer them;
    when they are in trouble, I will be with them.
    I will rescue them and honor them.
I will reward them with long life;
    I will save them" (TEV).

We join hands, his long, pencil-like fingers so wasted in disease, and we ascribe praise and thanksgiving to the God of the real world who replaces the air of death in a hospital room with the incense of His presence. We worship Him in that prayer, this God of praise, honor, glory, and power. And when I say the amen, we share a tear or two. But there is a new confidence in the eye of this sick man. He has forged a bit more of real-world faith and will fight on. This is real-world faith in action in the midst of a turbulent system.

It doesn't say so in the Scriptures, but my imagination pictures John climbing down his own version of a steel ladder. He has seen the Lord of glory, and he has heard the saints sing their praises in the direction of the throne. John is ready to go to work, and we are the recipients of his labor.

When Christ bids us follow and we accept His invitation, He invites us home, where we meet God. And what do we do? We worship. And the depth of our worship is in direct correlation with the strength of the real-world faith we forge. It's the first step, and it cannot be avoided.

For most of us, the word *worship* connects first with a corporate (or large group) experience, a meeting usually held in a church building under the direction of a pastor and church leaders. It is interesting, however, to sit with a group of Christ-followers and ask each person to describe the most memorable experience of corporate worship. My guess is that the majority will describe something outside a church building: a time about a campfire or at a retreat center, a hurried but intense experience under bombardment in combat, a spontaneous occasion in someone's home where Christ-followers got caught up in lots of joy.

And if you ask what happened that made it so memorable, you'll get answers such as these: we all sang songs that we knew; we all got to speak or read as we felt led; we felt free to open ourselves up to one another in the presence of the Lord; we felt strangely warmed by God's presence; we wept together, or we felt very free to laugh a lot; the prayers were unbelievably personal and tailored to where we were at; we simply forgot the clock. If my speculations are reasonably accurate, we all have some hard questions to ask about what goes on in most sanctuaries each week.

Every Christ-follower needs this involvement not as a spectator or a casual observer but as a full-fledged participant and a sometime leader. It is inconceivable to me that a serious Christ-follower could formulate a weekly schedule that did not include a corporate worship experience, for not only do we need it, but the Scriptures clearly command it and find ways to inform us that God's mighty men and women of both Testaments regularly pursued it themselves. Corporate worship services such as the one John witnessed in the Heavenlies are necessary to the forging of our real-world faith. They bring us in touch with the larger family of Christ-followers and remind us that we are not alone. They also nudge us to remember that in the Heavenly family there is no division of people into genders, ages, economies, races, or educations such as we are liable to experience during weekdays. We are one people in worship, and in that experience some of us are reduced to true size while others of us are elevated to true size: the true size that Jesus has designed for us.

If this is true, there is cause for alarm in the Christ-following community of our Western world because too many men and women professing to be Christ-followers are quietly (and sometimes not so quietly) protesting that their corporate worship experience is nearly meaningless. Ask them why they attend? Answer: fellowship; Sunday school is good for the kids; we've got to go somewhere; the pastor means well.

There are marvelous exceptions, of course. In almost every major city are those sanctuaries where something very powerful happens and people know that they have met God. One would not dare to identify these places with any particular denomination or worship culture. And one could not generalize and say that these places are small or large.

Let me be bold enough to say that every Christ-follower has a need for a corporate worship experience that invites him or her into the presence of a Holy God—an amazing, humbling gift. Every Christ-follower has a need for a corporate worship experience that expands the soul and rebukes and cleanses the guilt caused by indwelling evil. Every Christ-follower has a need to come to a place where he or she feels sensitively prayed for and where the Bible has been exposed in terms of its real-world relevance. Every Christ-follower has a need to feel that the worship service belongs to him or her and is not the possession of a few professionals who entertain us with their abilities at oratory and music.

Of course, with needs met there are responsibilities. Every Christ-follower has a responsibility to join the worship experience alert of mind and spirit, ready to participate with full enthusiasm in giving homage to God. Every Christ-follower has a responsibility to come with a heart open to conviction so that grace and forgiveness can be applied. Every Christ-follower has a responsibility to give generously as an act of thanksgiving and sacrifice to a kind God. Every Christ-follower has a responsibility to serve when it is appropriate. And every Christ-follower has a responsibility to open the heart and mind to learn when the chance comes to be fed on the Scriptures. Needs and responsibilities—it goes both ways.

Worship was never intended to be boring, nor was it meant to be an ordeal that one has to brace for each week. One is not helped to worship by being told that "it is not what you get out of it but what you put into it that counts." These are nice words, but they cannot overcome the reality of dreariness when a pastor or worship leaders do little to speak in a language people understand or provide forms of expression that reflect where the people are. You cannot squeeze blood from a stone, nor can you milk truth and motivation from an ill-prepared or poorly presented sermon. You cannot get caught up in a tune that makes the heart race with praise if the only people who can sing the tune are those with graduate degrees from the conservatory. And you cannot feel the sense of being protected by a prayer if the person who prays uses words and chooses topics demonstrating that he or she doesn't have the slightest idea about where you have been living.

If we permit ourselves to be led through meetings (which are called worship but really aren't) every Sunday that are irrelevant in terms of bringing us to God, helping us to face our real selves, and giving us enough courage to go back to the world as it really is, we have only ourselves to thank when our faith shrivels, our children drift from any desire to follow Jesus, and the folks beyond the church shrink from interest.

I fear that more than a few Christ-followers have given up on worship and simply plod through it as if it were a "dues" to be paid. We are not out of bounds if we ask the leaders of our corporate worship to think a bit harder about how to help us meet God in ways reflecting who we actually are as people and how we express ourselves. We are not being disrespectful if we ask that prayers and sermons and musical pieces make sense and that they reach into the mind and the heart and the emotions so that everyone's leading instincts of the spirit can be reasonably satisfied. We are not being unreasonable if we ask that our worship bring us to God so that we can walk out onto the streets confident that we know how to live as Christ-followers ought to live when the "bullets" fly on Monday morning.

I can hardly ever read the prison scene in Acts 16 without smiling. I see Paul and Silas chained up tight as can be. And what are they doing? (I know what I'd be doing!) They are worshiping. (I'm not sure I would have done that.) Singing, I believe the text says, well past midnight when most worship services in the Western world have long since ended. Although I love the great classical religious music of Bach and Mozart and the more recent music of composers like Randall Thompson, I must tell you that I do not think they sang that kind of music. Did they chant the psalms? Did they sing some of the first slogans and praise couplets that early Christ-followers were using and setting to local folk tunes? Probably!

I call them jailhouse songs: the kinds of melodies you can go out and hum all week long on subways, at desks, and while changing a baby. We need to challenge our worship leaders to give us the songs that we can sing in a jail. Some of us, someday, may end up in one. And some of us probably think we're already there. The corporate worship experience should be a springboard to the experience of personal worship. There is a sense in which what we did with brothers and sisters in the Christ-following family on the Lord's Day should be echoed in private (and sometimes with family) during the weekdays. Worship for a short time in the morning or in the evening; worship for a moment or two during the day when a pause in the action is in order.

A reading of Scriptures, a meditation from the spiritual classics, the humming of a jailhouse tune, a prayer of intercession and confession, a quiet period of thought as God's Spirit bathes the heart in Heavenly thoughts. Silence, solitude, peaceful reordering.

As we worship privately or corporately, we keep on forging a real-world faith because genuine worship in the presence of God reminds us that the world of the streets is not all there is to the real world. The Heavenlies were there before the streets, and they will be there long after the streets. *And the Heavenlies are where the real world begins.* Then we must forge a faith that knows how to operate there.

Years ago, Halford Lucock wrote of a doorman of a New York theater who had guarded the stage door for seventeen years but had never once entered the theater to see a performance. "Is it possible," Lucock asked,

> for a preacher and members of a congregation to become that sort of doorkeeper in the house of the Lord? The attention can be centered on the circumference, the incidental, the mechanical, and can be lost to the central living drama of salvation in individual lives and collective life which alone gives any meaning to the organization.

The man asks a worthy question.

THE REAL WORLD
OF THE INNER SELF

*To follow Christ is to master self
in the real world of the inner being
and give Him a gift
that may take a lifetime to produce
and that is Christlikeness*

CHAPTER TWELVE

Bedrock Thinking

A Thought for You, Smithy
What keeps a smithy going when the workday gets long? The energy deep within the heart. Smithy, have you looked lately to see what kind of reserves you have there? Make this inward look a high priority.

My boyhood was marked with the excitement of radio days. I thrilled to the adventures of Tom Mix, Sky King, the Green Hornet, the Shadow, and the Thin Man. But the most noble of them all, in my youthful estimation, was the Lone Ranger. His thrice-weekly adventures to save townspeople, ranchers, and Indians were events I simply refused to miss. I longed for the day when I too might be such a hero, so I engaged in rich fantasies in which I would come upon people in trouble, take charge, as did the Masked Man, and rescue them. In anticipation of that day I shadowboxed in front of the mirror, practiced a quick draw with my toy pistols, and reminded myself that when it came time to leave the scene of heroic action, like the Ranger, I would take no credit for what I'd achieved. I hasten to add that I was only nine years old when I did this.

The day came for me to live out my fantasy twenty years later. I was standing in a line with a friend in downtown St. Louis when we heard a woman's scream not more than a few hundred feet away. "Somebody get him" was what I heard next. And at about the same time I saw a young man sprinting along the sidewalk in my direction. He would pass where I was standing in about three seconds.

Was that a purse he was carrying? Why would a man be carrying a woman's purse? These and other kinds of questions poured through my mind in the first of those three seconds.

117

During second number two, I considered the appropriate action I might take *if* I decided to do anything. The Lone Ranger would have instinctively thrown himself into the man and banged him to the ground where people could hold him down until the police came. And it was clear that if I chose to act, this would be the best move.

But during the last of the three seconds, I thought about the consequences of that move. What if he had a weapon? What if no one assisted me once he was on the ground? And what if, in the collision of our bodies, I was hurt: hurt badly enough to be out of work for several weeks, hurt badly enough to be permanently injured, hurt badly enough to die? Was a woman's purse worthy of all this risk? Did the Lone Ranger wrestle with similar thoughts when he got ready to leap from his horse onto the back of a runaway outlaw? (Did the Lone Ranger have insurance?) Some of those questions occupied the third second of time in which I had to make my decision.

The decision was never made. Or to put it another way, indecision meant paralysis. The alleged purse snatcher galloped right on by, and my chance to be a hero in the fashion of the Masked Man was missed.

I don't think I've ever fantasized again about being a hero. That evening, I learned a distressing thing about myself. What one piece of me might wish to be—namely, a hero—is not what another piece—my cautious side—may permit. I do fervently hope that the next time my reaction in a crisis will be different, and I think about this a lot. But for reasons I don't fully understand, I—and everyone like me—am a highly complex person and not all the inner pieces are under suitable self-management all the time. So one can only hope for a better record should the occasion arise again.

According to the Bible, this complexity in the human condition that often leads to unpredictability or paralysis wasn't the way it was meant to be. I have the strong impression that the first man and woman enjoyed total control over their inner selves and thus could accomplish exactly what they wished. They knew themselves through and through, and they knew each other just as well. But a considerable amount of the control and self-knowledge they possessed must have been lost when evil plundered creation and wounded humanity. Ever since, one of the primary battles each person has fought is that of jousting with his body, his mind, and his spirit to assure that they will serve his best interests. One hears St. Paul cry out concerning the good things he would like to do but doesn't and the bad things he would like to avoid but does.

Probably one reason we love various kinds of sports, especially the solo performing sports such as skating and gymnastics, is that they give us a picture of what people can accomplish when they enjoy unusual control over their bodies and can accomplish such graceful achievements. I've often wondered if that wasn't part of Paul's attachment to sports because he uses athletic analogies on those occasions when he wants to talk about self-mastery or self-control.

This issue of mastering the inner self brings us back to the matter of forging a real-world faith.

The forging of a real-world faith means not only that one follows Christ into the Heavenlies to meet God, but that one follows Christ into the corridors of one's inner space in order to develop the spirit of Christlikeness. And Christlikeness in the inner life means an advancing knowledge of one's inner self and a growing ability to master it.

St. Paul has this notion in mind when he urges his protégé, Timothy, to greater self-mastery: "For God did not give us a spirit of timidity, but a spirit of power, of love and of self-discipline" (2 Tim. 1:7).

Again, as I said in earlier chapters, this concept of mastering oneself as a Christ-follower is often better observed than defined. And that is why I return once again to our friend Daniel. Few demonstrate this second dimension of real-world faith better than he.

Daniel's career record through the administrations of several pagan kings was remarkable. Any personnel file kept on him would have probably included notes about his candor, his consistency, his wisdom, and his adaptability to any circumstances.

We know little about his day-to-day management activities; we know more about several bold decisions of landmark significance, ones that could have cost him his career, if not his life, had they backfired on him. In each case Daniel was unflappable.

Unlike me, hesitating to do something that night in St. Louis, Daniel acted with confidence and without fear. What made the man tick?

Part of the answer seems to lie in two things you see Daniel doing consistently. He seems to have had an *alertness,* for example, toward anything that might inhibit him from bringing his body, his mind, and his deeper spirit under control—*his* control, not the king's or anyone else's.

And then you have to note the *positive disciplines* he practiced:

actions most busy people would probably have ignored. But they brought him strength and resolve, and when it was time to function like a hero (although I'm sure he wasn't aching for the opportunity), he did what was right, and his actions ended up being heroic.

I am impressed with several references to Daniel's management of himself that illustrate this.

The first has to do with his entrance, along with three companions also from Jerusalem, into the king's training school, something apparently akin to West Point or Sandhurst. A fringe benefit at the school was the unusually rich food and drink. It came from the king's kitchens and probably was served to acquaint the students with the sort of lifestyle they would enjoy in the future if they pressed themselves to achieve.

On this issue of diet Daniel first showed he would walk to the beat of a different drummer. He simply pushed his plate away. This action clearly upset the people responsible for the physical development of the students, and what ensued was a standoff eventuating in a ten-day experiment, during which Daniel and friends restricted themselves to a diet of vegetables and water. The diet does nothing for my imagination, but I admire their tenacity.

So what happened? The Bible records, "At the end of the ten days they looked healthier and better nourished than any of the young men who ate the royal food. So the guard took away their choice food and the wine they were to drink and gave them vegetables instead." The experiment was a success for Daniel, and it was the first indication that he would always be something of a "Lone Ranger" in the king's court.

The text from which this story comes concludes, "To these four young men God gave knowledge and understanding of all kinds of literature and learning. And Daniel could understand visions and dreams of all kinds" (Dan. 1:15–17).

This story has a purpose. It indicates that the future success of Daniel in the real world would have something to do with the attention he paid to bringing his personal life under control. The issue here is only food, but to Daniel and those of his faith, it was a big issue.

In some Christ-following traditions what Daniel did is called "separation," the choice to refrain from certain things because they are unhealthy to the body or the soul or because they reflect adversely on the cause of God's kingdom. I prefer to call what Daniel did "discipline" or "self-management." And why might he have practiced it?

Perhaps a practical reason first: he was somehow aware that to eat like that wasn't healthy. Second, he had chosen to live in accord with the traditions and laws of Jerusalem's lifestyle, not Babylon's. And third, he anticipated a standard of living in the king's service where self-management would be the only safeguard against self-destruction in an environment of indulgence and opulence. *In a world that might know very little about how to say no to self, Daniel would condition himself to do it with or without the help of others.*

Daniel's pursuit of self-management was not only a physical matter; it was also a matter of the spirit. In the royal administration of Darius, Daniel faced a crisis of loyalty between his worship of the God of Jerusalem and a newly declared state religion. He chose the former, even though the new law (designed by his adversaries to trip him up) stipulated the death penalty for violators.

> Now when Daniel learned that the decree had been published, he went home to his upstairs room where the windows opened toward Jerusalem. Three times a day he got down on his knees and prayed, giving thanks to his God, *just as he had done before.* Then these men went as a group and found Daniel praying and asking God for help (Dan. 6:10–11, emphasis mine).

One wonders if Daniel had his house specially designed with windows facing in the direction of Jerusalem so that he could carry out his thrice-daily discipline of prayer. From a practical standpoint, I don't know of any section in the entire book of Daniel that discloses the root of Daniel's success better than this one.

How did he survive and even thrive in a world of incredible brutality and disregard for human value? *He stopped everything three times a day and reoriented his spirit toward the God of Jerusalem.* Perhaps Daniel would tell us that the pressure of each day was so great that *not* to have prayed three times a day would have guaranteed personal catastrophe. But he was not going to give ground to attempted intimidation, just as he had not bowed to the pressure of life at the king's table years earlier.

These comments indicate that Daniel's enemies knew of his daily pattern of spiritual activity. Knowing just how predictable he was in such matters made it possible for them to design a legal process that could be turned against him. Isn't it ironic! They were going to use the very thing that had made him effective for Babylonian interests to gain their desired ends: namely, to do the man in. Today they call that the dark side of politics.

Most everyone knows how the matter came to a head: Daniel went to the lions' den and came out well rested the next day. By order of the king, his adversaries involuntarily visited the lions' den soon after but were not as fortunate. I have never heard anyone observe that the turn of events in which his enemies (and their families) died instead of him is one more example of the cruel, cruel world in which Daniel lived.

So at the beginning of Daniel's Babylonian life and toward the end of it, we learn an important principle: the man was in charge of his own life. He was his own person; rather, he was God's person and managed himself in accord with God's laws.

Whether it was food for the stomach or prayer for the soul, Daniel was in charge. This is a mark of real-world faith.

Is there any other key to this practice of self-management or self-mastery? I believe there is, and it is revealed in the text of Daniel's long prayer:

> O Lord, the great and awesome God, who keeps his covenant of love with all who love him and obey his commands, *we have sinned and done wrong. We have been wicked and have rebelled; we have turned away from your commands and laws. We have not listened to your servants the prophets*. . . . Lord, you are righteous, but this day we are covered with shame. . . . The Lord our God is merciful and forgiving, even though we have rebelled against him; we have not obeyed the LORD our God or kept the laws he gave us through his servants the prophets. All Israel has transgressed your law and turned away, refusing to obey you. . . . Our sins and the iniquities of our fathers have made Jerusalem and your people an object of scorn to all those around us (Dan. 9:4–16, emphasis mine).

Here is theology (the knowledge of God) mixed with anthropology (the knowledge of humanity). In this case it is Daniel looking deep within his own being and identifying *the condition of spirit* that had plagued every generation of his people: the matter of indwelling evil. This is a prayer of repentance.

If evil is not exposed, identified, and offered up in an act of repentance, self-mastery of the kind that marked Daniel cannot occur. The prayer high-profiles a quality in Daniel that should not be ignored. *The man was not afraid to look within and acknowledge that there were*

things in need of repentance and that before the great qualities of perfor-
mance could be recognized, these unfortunate qualities had to be dealt
with.

As I said earlier, this is part of what Christ-following is all about.
When we choose to follow and to commence the forging of a real-world
faith, Christ leads us deep into ourselves, offering a process in which
an interior renovation of inner space might begin. It is not always a
happy experience until the end when we see what has resulted. There
can be embarrassment, struggle, and failure. But this simply has to
happen if the faith of Daniel is to be ours in our real world.

That's why Daniel was a hero on the streets of Babylon and why I
was not a hero for an evening on the streets of St. Louis. He knew
himself; I didn't. He prepared for the moments of testing; I didn't. He
disciplined himself; I shadowboxed. He pursued a fervent, regular intercessory life; I fooled with toys. He anticipated the issues of his
time; I was surprised by them. He willingly explored the weaknesses
within his spirit; I preferred the fantasies.

Of course it is absurd to make any serious comparison between a
statesman running a government and a young man debating whether
or not he should mow down a purse-snatcher. But then again, the
principles that make us ready for any contingency may not be too dis-
similar.

The person who forges a real-world faith gets very serious about
looking deep within and bringing the scattered pieces of self together
in Christlikeness. You see the results in a man like Daniel.

CHAPTER THIRTEEN

A Spoiled Species

On a recent summer evening, I sat out on the balcony of our New York apartment and scanned the East River with my binoculars for something interesting. In the lens I caught the sight of a green van pulling off to the side of the FDR Drive, which is located across the river from where we live. I watched as the driver got out and raised the hood. He was obviously having a problem with his engine.

Occasionally I would pick up the binoculars and check on the man and his green van to see if he had managed to find the source of his trouble. He hadn't, and after about an hour, I saw him gather a few things from the inside of the vehicle and begin walking down the road. If it has occurred to you to wonder why I would not offer help, it might be helpful to note that to go from where I live to the other side of the East River where the van was parked would have taken almost an hour.

The next morning I noticed that the green van was still where its driver had left it, and I wondered why he had not returned to fix it or tow it away. New Yorkers know that it is not smart to leave an unattended vehicle for long in a place like that.

When I came home that evening, I again noted the van's presence on the FDR Drive. At the same moment that I was looking, an automobile pulled up behind the van, and its driver got out. *He's come to get his van started,* I said to myself, and I picked up my binoculars to see what he would do.

I watched as the man peered through the windows of the van (as if he'd never seen it before), then cautiously opened the front door on the passenger side and climbed in. I could see him remove what must have been a tool from his pocket and work on something on the dashboard. About ninety seconds later he jumped from the van and ran toward his car with something under his arm. My field glasses were just good enough for me to see what it was. He hadn't fixed anything; he had stolen the van's radio! (Ninety seconds was all it took. I once took four hours to remove the radio in my car.)

Later in the evening, I saw another car drive up behind the green van. This time two men got out and quickly studied it as the first man who'd taken the radio had done. One of them went back to his own car and reappeared with a jack. Within minutes they were gone with two of the van's tires. The time-conscious race drivers at Indianapolis would have drooled over their speedy tire-changing skills.

When I awakened the following morning, the green van came to mind, and I looked once again in its direction. Now a door was missing, and I could see through the opening that the front seat had been removed. That evening another examination revealed that the window glass was gone. And the next morning when I made what was becoming my habitual inspection, I discovered (and I write this with a kind of admiration) that the hood was raised *and the engine was missing.*

All that remained of the green van was the frame. Tires, glass, seats, and now the engine were gone. It sat there on its wheel drums, looking like a beached whale.

There's a story there, I muttered, as I left for an early morning breakfast. I found myself wondering about the day that the green van had been driven away from some dealer's showroom by a proud owner. A beautiful green van, fully equipped, ready for business, for family outings, for cross-country trips. But that was then. And now it was picked clean, a worthless hulk on the curb of the FDR Drive.

And I thought of a world, once brand-new, brought forth and held together by the energized word of God. A world into which two beautiful people were introduced: people with astonishing capacities, made, as the Scriptures put it, in the image of their Maker.

I pondered the world today and felt that both creation and humanity were somewhat reminiscent of the stripped green van. War, drugs, crime, environmental exploitation, racism, greed, oppressive governments—the list of ways in which creation and humanity have been raped and pillaged is endless.

The biblical view of creation tells us that when God made the Heavens and the earth, all things existed in a design of order and harmony. The first human beings lived in that state for an undetermined period of time. Dominion (I prefer to say management responsibility) over the earth was delegated to Adam and Eve. You could say that creation was theirs to discover and enjoy, to learn the infinite number of ways in which everything reflected the genius and glory of its Designer.

The order and harmony were shattered, however, the day Adam and Eve decided to challenge God's word. From that point on, an evil spirit polluted the world, introducing random disorder and confusion. Truth was no longer obvious; deceit became humanity's number one problem. Instead of certainties, there were only probabilities; instead of clarities, there were only estimates. Creation was no longer man's servant, certainly not his friend; it became his competitor, and down through history, each—creation and humanity—has beat the other to a pulp at one time or another.

From the Brazilian forests falling before chain saws to the oil spills blanketing ocean shores, from the dwindling ozone layers to the toxic waste dumps, humanity is beating creation to a slow death. And the mystery behind this all is that humanity knows what it is doing. It has all the evidence that intelligent people need to conclude that life as we know it on this planet is headed toward a catastrophe.

To put it rather blandly, since the fall of man in the Garden, much of life has ceased to be fun except for certain unusual moments. And even those unusual moments are not necessarily the possession of every person or generation. Death has become the all-pervading reality that the younger ignore only for a while and the older cannot long neglect: death, this mind-boggling, universal reality that was never meant to be.

It probably never occurred to the owner of the green van, when he first purchased it, that his beautiful, peppy vehicle would end its days by the side of a main New York City thoroughfare being picked apart as a dead carcass is dismantled by vultures or hyenas. I don't suppose it ever occurred to the first man and woman that choices they made would introduce powers to the world that would eventuate in its slow deterioration and demise either.

C. S. Lewis in his book *The Problem of Pain* speculated on the deterioration of humanity and creation. Speaking of the tragedy of man, Lewis wrote, "Man is now a horror to God and to himself and a creature ill-adapted to the universe not because God made him so but because he has made himself so by the abuse of his free will."

Lewis went on to speak of humanity in the original creation state. Total self-control or self-mastery was the order of the day; that is, it was so until the great act of disobedience:

> Up to that moment the human spirit had been in full control of the human organism. It doubtless expected that it would retain this control when it had ceased to obey God. But its authority over the organism was a delegated authority which it lost when it ceased to be God's delegate.
>
> . . . our present condition, then, is explained by the fact that we are members of a spoiled species.

This "spoiledness" is a major theme of the Bible. From the moment that creation's calm was ruptured by the violence of evil, God embarked on a mission of reclamation. My sense of logic causes me to wonder why He didn't melt the whole mess down and start all over again. But He didn't. God's mission seems to be twofold: redeeming the human race, first, and remaking creation, second.

The coming of Jesus was the centerpiece of God's reclamation plan. And as the Son of God intersected with various kinds of human beings, marvelous things happened. He set people free! Lives marked with all the effects of evil's strength were refurbished from the inside out.

That's what draws many of us to Jesus: the changes He caused in the human experience of simple, plain people like us. We read the stories over and over again and evoke hope from them, a sense that the healing and restoration we hear about can be ours.

In each case of reclamation we see a transition from a condition of personal enslavement—some call it bondage—to a condition of increasing self-mastery or self-management: becoming again what God originally designed a human being to be.

Wherever Jesus went among people, He pinpointed servitude to evil power, sickness, fear, handicaps, superstition, and spiritual numbness. Self-mastery meant transiting from these forms of entrapment to a freedom of the inner life and regaining some original faculties of management of one's piece of the creation.

We have only a smattering of diverse stories that feature the changes in people's lives. St. John writes enthusiastically that "if every one of them [the things Jesus did] were written down, I suppose that even the whole world would not have room for the books that would be written" (John 21:25). On the other hand, we also learn of communities such as Nazareth, Jesus' boyhood town, which utterly rejected Him and saw virtually nothing of this power He possessed to restore brokenness.

The opening condition for someone to experience the liberating power of Jesus was the person's willingness to acknowledge that he was a part of the spoiled species and that he needed deliverance from evil's bondage. That is what the Bible refers to as repentance: an act of self-disclosure and a choice to change direction and allegiance in life. Some also refer to this as conversion.

Not everyone was prepared to deal like that. Cover-up of the inner fact of spoiledness, the opposite of repentance, was a way of life to many, then and now. A fierce arrogance prevailed in the breast of more than one person, a conviction that enough time, enough thinking, and enough effort could rectify one's personal situation without resorting to any kind of self-disclosure.

When Jesus first left the carpenter shop and engaged in the activities of an itinerant teacher, He quickly polarized people because He insisted on that self-disclosure. The extremes with which people reacted to Him were soon obvious: those who opened their inner lives to Him and those who slammed the door shut telling Him, in effect, to mind His own business.

Again, the issue was the inner life that must be exposed. More than a few were willing to open their minds to Him in order to debate and compare notes. Many of them, I'm sure, would have been happy to follow in His train if the issues had been cerebral. But minds were not Jesus' number one target; inner lives, the hearts of people, were.

Then again many people were willing to open their mouths to the -Lord. They'd have been willing to admit to their poverty if He were to reciprocate by offering a little bread for the stomach and a little healing for sick bodies. But again, the stomach was not first on Jesus' agenda.

But opening the spirit or the heart—that's another matter. The mind fools with ideas; the body with food and drink. But the spirit? That is where the self really gets exposed. The values, the motives (ulterior and forthright), the attitudes, the guilt, and the ambitions. This is not an area many of us, then or now, are comfortable revealing to anyone. I'm not sure it's an area we're comfortable exploring to much depth ourselves. This is the place, the heart, where the original fall of man actually happened. The overt actions were only the logical result.

And that is the problem people had with Jesus. They were used to the folks who wanted to play mind games with religion or politics, and He wouldn't play. What unnerved some was His astonishing ability to see right into people and tell them things about themselves that either they didn't know or they had been trying to cover up so that no one else would know.

One man in the Bible, simply called "the rich young man" (would we dare refer to him today as a yuppie?), is a case in point. He came to Jesus anticipating a marvelous discussion on the issue of eternal life and its acquisition. He was well-armed with a resume of righteous claims of behavior, and he played his card early in the conversation. But the Lord looked deep within the spirit (Scripture says, "Jesus looked at him and loved him") and challenged him about his real obsession: his holdings. The game was over, and the fellow went away "sad, because he had great wealth" (Mark 10:17–22). It was not a good day for self-disclosure.

One can get away with nothing if he is in the presence of someone who can scour the inner being and surface what's there. The leading religious party members of the day quickly labeled Jesus an adversary because He had the capacity to do the one thing that terrified them most: expose the inner person. They were reasonably good people, but they put a premium on decorating the exterior of life with words, robes, and rituals and camouflaging the interior of life where the scenery was spoiled.

But others were actually drawn to Him because they sensed an overriding safety in being transparent with Him. Instead of heaping shame upon them as others did, He gave grace. That's it: self-disclosure always resulted in grace in the presence of Jesus. And grace meant reclamation from spoiledness. Grace meant a new start.

A letter sits on my desk from a person who is in deep personal remorse over a matter that has gone wrong in life. This person is closely associated with a well-known Christian personality who has expressed strong, unyielding opinions about what should happen if people fail in certain ways. Who can I turn to and where can I find help, the letter writer asks, when I already know that there is no way back in my colleague's mind? This "leader" will apparently never know that in his circle of friends is one who lives every day with a broken heart that may not ever be revealed because of the fear there may be no grace in self-exposure.

As I read the letter, I find myself grateful that no one ever found Jesus to be close-minded if he was openhearted. No one ever found the future blocked when he repented of the past. The Lord's gentleness in the moment of one's self-disclosure is among the most remarkable things about Him.

A powerful example of this is Zacchaeus, the Jericho tax collector who climbed a tree to be above the crowd and get a glimpse of Jesus. Why did the Lord stop and choose to visit at Zacchaeus's house that day? It's clear that He saw what no one else could see: the man known for his exploitation of people was ready to acknowledge the inner spoiledness that, in this case, was out-and-out greed. The grace of Christ was drawn to the openness of the sinner.

What is the point of all this? That Christ-following always involves exposure and renovation of the inner life. And not just a small part of the inner life, but an ever-enlarging section of it. Let me reformulate the principle of this section:

The real world is not only that place called Heaven where a person meets God and worships, but it is the place called the heart where a person is caused by Christ-following to look within and regain the power to master himself and reflect the genius of his Maker.

In another book, *Rebuilding Your Broken World,* I have tried to make the point, which is hardly novel or original, that the inner space of a person is as infinite as outer space. That's a lot to explore and a lot to renovate. Perhaps it takes an eternity to discover what is there and what has been distorted and reduced to chaos by evil. But it seems clear that the choice to follow Jesus means the exploration has begun. To say I follow Him and yet resist this process of exploration He initiates is to neutralize the means of forging a real-world faith.

Hardly a day goes by that I do not see the great Queensboro Bridge spanning the East River between Long Island and Manhattan in New York City. This double-decked bridge carries thousands of cars in and out of Manhattan every day. There is a work crew whose constant task is to maintain that bridge. They inspect every one of its cables, its great steel girders, and its roadways. They are constantly searching for rust and structural deterioration. Inspection never ceases. Repair is always underway. I am glad for the vigilance of that crew, especially on the occasions when I drive on the bridge.

Not long ago the Williamsburg Bridge, a sister bridge down the river from the Queensboro, was closed for six months because of structural deterioration. The city had not made its maintenance a priority and had cut the money from the operating budget that would have spotted the corrosion and done something about it. The result? Six months of traffic jams and commuter inconvenience. Call it "spoiledness": what happens to a bridge or a person when exposure in the inner parts is ignored.

I do not write lightly about the personal self-disclosure of spoiledness. It has been a major theme in my life in the recent past. It became that because a neglect of inner corrosion caused a disruption of everything important to me. I was forced to enter into deep self-examination as to what had happened and why. Like the Williamsburg Bridge, I had to virtually close down the "traffic" of my life for a while until repairs were made.

It did not take long for me to realize that I had blindly walked into a trap common to many people. I had permitted myself to become so busy, so absorbed in projects that had value in themselves, and so responsive to all the good things people suggested I undertake that I lost touch with the depths of my inner person.

I do not blame either people or the system in which I then lived for my choices. I blame my own blindness, my personal resistance to self-disclosure. If at that time I had followed Jesus, as indeed I should have, into my inner being, as I now believe He wanted to lead me, I would have spotted the insidious spoiling energies forming like an inflammable gas within and, perhaps, dealt with them before they exploded so painfully. But I didn't follow Jesus then; I was too busy assuming that He wanted me to follow Him out into the religious world where there seemed to be so many opportunities to do so many wonderful things. One cannot afford such a stupid choice too many times. Once is more than enough.

This kind of blindness may be one of the scandals of modern faith. It seduces us into thinking that our value is in the many things we can accomplish. And the more we accomplish, the more the praise of well-meaning people enforces the idea that a bit more accomplishment will be even better. But the price of increased doing is the parallel loss of being able to live at the deeper inner levels.

I will never fully understand the mechanics of the process, but now

I look back and realize that somewhere, for a short period of time, I lost touch with myself in my ever-expanding efforts to be in touch with others. And a part of me that was related to the spoiledness of which C. S. Lewis speaks became unmanaged enough to unleash the disorder leading to much sadness.

To repeat then, Christ-following means in part the process of going within to the deep inner world that is dark and chaotic. Humankind has done some credible things in the outer, visible world, but it has done almost nothing to descend into the depths of the inner, personal world and discover what Paul Tournier once called the violence within:

> In contrast with my illustrious fellow-citizen Jean-Jacques Rousseau, who thought that man was by nature good, and perverted only by society, I think that he is violent by nature and that he is preserved from the worst effects of his violence by society, though at times it stirs up and exploits his cruel instincts. As Denis de Roughmont has remarked, "the atom bomb is not in the least dangerous. It is a thing. What is fearfully dangerous is man." To that I add these three quotations from Dr. Anthony Storr: "We are the cruelest and most ruthless species that has ever walked the earth." "It is a mistake to believe that the ordinary man is not capable of the extremes of cruelty." "Each one of us harbors within himself those same savage impulses which lead to murder, to torture, and to war." Really to understand that is to stop passing judgment on our fellows. *(The Violence Within)*

We spoiled it—creation, that is—all of us! The creation seen in our outer space, and the creation in our inner space. In one simple decision made by our father Adam (but really by all of us), we exchanged the incredible privilege of managing creation for a battlefield of inner and outer conflicts that grow more complex.

Christ invites us to follow Him and take a hard look at the inner life where this decision is effectively made. Acknowledging the spoiledness and permitting Him to reclaim it are parts of the process of forging a real-world faith.

CHAPTER FOURTEEN

The CAT Scan

Look right there," the physician pointed with the dull end of his pencil at an X ray on the lighted wall. "See that circle? That's a healthy nerve. Now see this point here? No circle. Right? That's why you're hurting." I would never have spotted it myself, but when the expert pointed it out, I saw immediately how the disk in my back was bulging and putting the squeeze on a root of the sciatic nerve, which in turn was sending unnatural signals down my left leg.

I was in the office of a surgeon who specializes in backs, and he was telling me why mine was giving me trouble. Earlier I had been put through the CAT scan at the hospital, an experience akin to being rolled through a large doughnut while your insides are being photographed from every angle. Now we were looking at the pictures.

It felt strange to be looking at bones, disks, and nerves inside my body. But I was grateful to know why I'd been in pain for six months and what could be done about it. For some time, I'd been putting off this visit, afraid that I would be told I needed surgery. But finally the discomfort was great enough to force me to do what I'd been resisting. And now I knew: unless the disk shrank by itself, surgery was inevitable.

A condition inside my body was controlling me. I was aware of it every time I moved. I never rose from a chair or got out of bed or my

133

car that I did not give careful attention to whatever it was within me causing the pain.

Now I knew what the condition actually was and what would have to be done about it. The CAT scan and the physician's expertise in reading it had told me what I needed to know.

The great biblical passage on spiritual CAT scans, if you please, is Psalm 139. I like to think that David, king of Israel, wrote it. Traditional biblical scholars liked that notion too. But contemporary students of the Bible are not so sure.

My argument for David's authorship is hardly scholarly. It just seems like the sort of thing he would write. Authors tend to be drawn to subjects with which they personally struggle, and this psalm is in part a meditation or prayer about deceit and its need to be exposed. By nature, David was a deceitful man, and it would not surprise me if he would take on such a topic with an eye toward dealing with his own problems.

The psalm opens with a blunt statement about God's habit of CAT scanning the human spirit:

> O LORD, you have searched me
> and you know me.
> You know when I sit and when I rise;
> you perceive my thoughts from afar.
> You discern my going out and my lying down;
> you are familiar with all my ways.
> Before a word is on my tongue
> you know it completely, O LORD.
> You hem me in—behind and before;
> you have laid your hand upon me.
> Such knowledge is too wonderful for me,
> too lofty for me to attain.

As I said, the point of this poem is inner exposure, the darkness of the human heart forced into the light so that some hidden things can finally be identified and dealt with. The ultimate goal? The psalmist will say it in the last words of the poem: that he might travel in the "way everlasting." In New Testament terminology, that's Christ-following.

One could gain increasing self-mastery *if* he could first identify those controlling inner energies and motivations at the root of behaviors and attitudes that the psalmist labels wicked and offensive. The thing impressing the psalmist enough to pick up the pen is that the Everlasting God does indeed identify those inner energies and motivations of the heart in a way far beyond our ability to discern them. It is a deep exposure of self, which is, as he says, "too wonderful, too lofty" for us to attain. Therefore, relationship with God and the forging of a faith of any value will involve dealing with such heart-oriented information. As I have said, the real world does not begin in the streets; it also reaches to the Heavenlies and to the depths—the darkest depths—of the human heart.

What is being said here is utterly consistent with what we saw in the behavior of Jesus when He walked among people and penetrated the depths of their hearts also. He told them things about themselves that they could only guess at on their own.

This was reflected in my situation when I went to the back surgeon. The knowledge of the cause of my back problem was beyond me; I could only react to the pain. It took an expert to read the pictures for me and tell me what the pain meant. And when one follows Christ into the inner life, a similar thing occurs. Just as the psalmist looked to God for aid in self-exposure, so the Christ-follower looks for help to seek the things preventing the forging of real-world faith.

The "CAT scan" psalm moves ahead (you may wish to stop and read its full length) to celebrate this expert knowledge of the inner being that God possesses. This is a God who knows all things, so He can't be fooled, the writer says. He is also present everywhere, so we can't hide from Him (as Jonah tried to do). And He is limitless in power as demonstrated in His creation of the psalmist himself and therefore cannot be overthrown.

All of this leaves the psalmist feeling rather defenseless should he wish to continue his deceptive habits: "How precious to me are your thoughts, O God! How vast is the sum of them!"

How can anything be withheld from a God like this? This is a disturbing thought to a man—if it's David—who had been so good at lying to himself, to others, and apparently—so he'd thought—to God.

When the psalm ends, the writer capitulates. It's as if he finally concludes that if God is going to look within—like it or not—he may as well cooperate with the process and invite the examination leading to self-disclosure:

Search me, O God, and know my heart;
test me and know my anxious thoughts.
See if there is any offensive way in me,
and lead me in the way everlasting.

This is the prayer of one who seeks to forge a real-world faith. It is
the Christ-follower saying, I choose to follow the Lord into the darkness of my private world. I anticipate being chagrined over what we
are likely to find together, but I will face it *if* He will treat it with grace.
And of course, He has promised to do that.

This search is the discipline that I believe must be exercised with
consistent resolve. It is the search to the most profound depths
within. It's a thoroughly morbid affair and better to be avoided, were it
not that our Guide is so full of loving kindness, far more gentle than we
are with one another and even with ourselves.

What has come to me with great force as I have wrestled with the
development of my faith is my ineptitude in engaging in such self-
exposure. Let's face it: one part of the self keeps secrets from the
other part. I imagine my conscious self saying to my heart, *What are
you really thinking?* and hearing that darker part respond, *You don't
really want to know, and I wouldn't tell you anyway.*

As I write this, I can look out my window and see the great Empire
State Building with its 102 floors. That enormous skyscraper is a
workplace for thousands of people each day. And although at this distance, it looks like a rather monolithic structure, I know that on every
floor there is a maelstrom of activity, people rushing to and fro: buying, selling, arguing, competing, innovating, succeeding and failing.

My private world is a place like the Empire State Building with its
flurry of motion. I may be aware of what is happening on certain floors
of my heart, but I am stupefied when I discover that other things are
occurring on different floors. What may look beautiful and good on
floor 35 within me is more than offset by something ugly and slander-
ous on floor 62. Only the Divine Architect—who made the psalmist
and me—knows what is happening on every floor simultaneously.

St. Paul was mystified by the complexities of the multistoried
structure within, and he yelled out, "O wretched man that I am! Who
will deliver me from this body of death?" (Rom. 7:24 NKJV). He
needed constant self-exposure, and he knew he needed deliverance
from what attempted to control him and bar the way to Christlikeness.
Me too!

It is possible to reduce our view of the darkness within to a carefully contrived list of sinful behaviors and, when that happens, to fall into the tendency to grade them (denying all the time that we do) so that there are number nine or ten sins (on a scale of ten), which we deem to be virtually unforgivable, and number one or two sins, which we excuse with barely a thought. Better that for a short time we set aside our lists of what is truly wicked or merely excusable in order to look beneath the actions to the darker controlling conditions at the root of those behaviors. Again and again that is what Jesus did. He dealt with the causes, the subterranean furies within the human heart that energized the sinful choices people made.

I think the most prolific example of this is Jesus' treatment of the men who brought a woman to Him who had been caught in the act of adultery. They demanded to know what justice He would give her.

On a purely behavioral level, she was indeed the worst person in the circle. This was a number nine or ten sin on the scale used in that day, and there was no question about what she deserved. That Jesus didn't speak to her sin immediately must not lead us to assume that He was ignoring the seriousness of what she had done.

Anybody could have dealt with the issue of her behavior. That knowledge wasn't so "wonderful," to use the psalmist's language. But Christ turned on the CAT scan and disclosed the heart of darkness that existed in equal intensity all about the circle: prostitute *and* Pharisee. Her accusers wanted to highlight overt behavior; Christ brought everyone to a point of humiliation when He chose to focus on the covert conditions, the controlling elements, of the heart. Suddenly, everyone was on the defensive. That's why they all left: the older first and the younger. He had forced self-exposure, and self-exposure to anyone who thinks like a Pharisee is like repellent to a mosquito.

Forging a real-world faith, then, means that our version of reality must extend inward, naming the controlling elements within. In naming them, we can begin the process of inner liberation: offering it to the One who deals with it in forgiveness and gives the resolve to beat it.

How does this happen? For many, it is first a meditative process in which one senses the finger of Christ writing upon the conscious mind the inner issues that need to be fully explored and, when necessary, rebuked.

It is also a process driven by Scripture study. As we bathe our minds in the holy writings, some things seem to fairly leap out and connect with realities within. We see ourselves in the behaviors of biblical personalities or in the teachings of the apostles and prophets. A command from the lips of the Lord suddenly cuts to the bone, and we know that self-exposure has occurred.

We need the relationships of special brothers and sisters who are Christ-followers to engage in self-exposure. The pastoral function is a caring matter before it is descriptive of a professional activity. God frequently gives us pastoral friends to gently lead us toward insight if we are willing to listen and accept truth spoken in love.

Self-exposure can also come as we carefully examine the consequences of our actions, as each of us asks, What drives me to think, or act, or say things in certain ways? What is the meaning of my attitudes and motivations? God honors the person who asks hard questions of himself and will not ignore the honest inquiry.

And what might be some categories we ought to be watching most closely in terms of avoiding control and gaining self-mastery?

The Christ-follower asks tough questions about how controlled he is by people. Is he a people-pleaser because he wants to feel valuable on the basis of people's opinions? Does he use people rather than build them in order to achieve his objectives? Does he harbor resentment against people, or is he controlled by competition or jealousy against people?

The Christ-follower takes a careful look at his connection to material things. Does he compute his value as a person by how much he owns? Is money ever a controlling matter? Is there a temptation to think of security in terms of the amount of money in the bank? Can one say no to the purchase of things when there is no serious need? Is one generous, able to give a significant part of what one earns to those who are not so fortunate? Is there a tendency to judge others by what they own?

The Christ-follower takes inventory of his fantasies, the condition of his thought-life. What drives his thoughts? Is he captivated by frequent imaginations of immoral behavior? What about attitudes toward pornography? Is there obsession about being someone he is not? Or constant dissatisfaction over one's place in life?

Looking within, the Christ-follower seeks the evidence of unresolved guilt. And when there is guilt, what is it saying? Are there matters of the past that need to be resolved and restitution made? Are there issues in one's life, which God's Spirit is trying to raise through inner feelings of uneasiness, that need to be faced?

The Christ-follower will want to look within to monitor attitudes toward career. What is one working for? Is the work being done with excellence? Is work unnaturally controlling one's life? And what is the attitude toward leisure and play? Is it recreation? Is it healthy to the spirit? Does it make one grow?

And what of memories, especially ones marked with great pain and anger? Has he granted forgiveness to important people in the past who have wronged him? Is he controlled by defeats or failures from other years that prohibit him from making strides forward today?

Are habit patterns, addictions, and affections controlling him and making it impossible for him to pursue the Christlike lifestyle he believes God has called him to? Where might he need the help of a brother or a sister in accountability for these things? Where might he need the assistance of a counselor or a pastor who could help him put his finger on the sources of his captivity?

These are the sorts of categories and questions the forger of real-world faith pursues. And he quickly learns that this pursuit of inner self-disclosure is a constant discipline. When it is ignored, self-mastery is slowly but surely lost.

We can assume that each of us has controlling powers within that have to be identified and rebuked in the wonderful strength God gives. But this is a daily search, and it happens only when the forger of real-world faith thinks it serious enough to take time to do the inner homework.

I began this chapter with a visit to my back surgeon. And I recalled his ability to read the pictures and show the hidden me (at least that part of me called the backbone) to myself. I had to have his help. All I knew was that I was experiencing great discomfort, and it was jeopardizing many projects I had in mind, including the writing of this book.

No one can forge a real-world faith without following Christ, the gracious Doctor, into the dark recesses of the inner spirit. And this is not a function of spiritual life that most of us are likely to permit with ease. We have too much to hide, too much that we are embarrassed about.

The grim reality is that either these things are exposed now when they can be dealt with in grace and restoration or they will be exposed in that frankly frightening day, as St. Paul describes it, "when God will judge men's secrets through Jesus Christ" (Rom. 2:16).

The great objective of following Christ into the inner world of the spirit is to expose those things creating bondage and the associated loss of self-mastery. As the back surgeon did for me, so we are likely to hear Christ say to us in one way or another, See this? This is what it ought to look like. See this? There's your trouble.

The deeper we go in following Him, the darker it gets, the more frightening it gets, the more humbling it becomes. The great saints learned that the closer one walks to Christ, the more evil one discovers within.

One of England's great eighteenth-century pastors, Henry Venn, wrote, "I began to keep my diary hoping to find myself in everything exact, and almost without fault; how was I surprised and ashamed when innumerable deficiencies and blots and corruption appeared." What Venn discovered was predictable, even for an English divine. It happens every time we follow Christ far enough within.

Lest I permit this chapter to end on something of a gloomy note, let me urge readers forward. The journey to the inner depths that Christ initiates may have its dark, disappointing moments. But the very fact that we are willing to make this journey and the very fact that we are appalled at what we find (as was Henry Venn) powerfully indicate that God is actively working in the real world of our hearts.

Years ago Gail and I toured a village in Liberia that had been built for men and women suffering from Hansen's disease, an illness better known in past times as leprosy. We visited with memorable men and women who had suffered greatly from this disease, which deadens the nerves and makes it impossible to feel pain. That lack of pain sensation causes the loss of fingers and toes, for example. One does not feel the burn of the fire or the bite of the snake, and so infection is able to create its physical havoc before one is aware of a problem. When I learned this, I became aware that not to be able to feel pain is a serious matter. Pain is actually a gift.

The pain that comes when we walk with Christ through the inner self is a gift. It tells us that there is life within, and that hope and possibility for the future exist. Daniel became the man we know him to be because he was not afraid to deal with the pain of the heart. It was a threshold, he saw, to grace and new growth. And that's what we want to see as we forge this real-world faith that makes us increasingly like Christ.

CHAPTER FIFTEEN

Recovery

A Thought for You, Smithy

If your faith building gets into trouble, Smithy, stop everything for as long as it takes to understand what went wrong. But knowing what happened is not enough. Ask yourself what can be done to substitute wrong actions with right ones. There's no need to repeat destructive history.

In his book *The Sacred Journey*, Frederick Buechner writes of an evening when he journeyed to his mother's New York City apartment for dinner. "It was to be just the two of us," Buechner says, "and we had both looked forward to it, not simply as mother and son but as two old friends who no longer got to see each other all that much."

Just as they were sitting down to what was obviously a carefully planned meal and a beautifully decorated table, the phone rang. The call was for Buechner, and it came from a teaching colleague. "He had not spoken more than a word or two when his voice broke, and I realized to my horror that he was weeping," Buechner states. The caller went on to explain that his parents and his pregnant sister had been involved in a serious automobile accident on the West Coast, and their chances for recovery were doubtful. He was at the airport preparing to fly to them, and he was so distraught that he wondered if Buechner could come and sit with him until the plane departed.

Buechner writes that he was torn as to what he should do:

> My instinct . . . was to be nothing so much as afraid. I was afraid of my friend's fear and of his tears. I was afraid of his faith that I could somehow be a comfort and help to him and afraid that I was not friend enough to be able to be. . . .
>
> So although I knew as well as anybody that I had no choice but

141

to say that I would come, what I said instead, Heaven help me, was that I would come if I possibly could, but there were things I had to take care of first and would he phone me back in about ten minutes.

His return to his mother's dinner table was not a happy one. He describes her annoyance over the intrusive phone call and her insistence that her son not go to the airport, that his friend's request was unreasonable and juvenile, and that her son ought not to let anyone ruin the evening the two of them had been planning for a long time.

Everything she said was precisely what at some level of my being I had already been saying to myself, and that was of course what made it so appalling. It was only when I heard it on someone else's lips that I heard it for what it was, and as much out of revulsion at myself as out of pity for my friend, I resolved that as soon as he called again, I would tell him that I would come immediately.

But he never went because when his friend called back, he informed Buechner that he was doing better and that it would not be necessary to come at all. "The consequence was that I did not go . . . and such as it was my mother and I had our evening together after all." Frederick Buechner's conclusion to the story caught my attention:

My mother's apartment by candlelight was haven and home and shelter from everything in the world that seemed dangerous and a threat to my peace. And my friend's broken voice on the phone was a voice calling me out into that dangerous world not simply for his sake, as I suddenly saw, but also for my sake. The shattering revelation of that moment was that true peace, the high and bidding peace that passeth all understanding, is to be had not in retreat from the battle, but only in the thick of battle.

I find Frederick Buechner's self-exposure and his conclusion a remarkable piece of writing. It is a perfect example of the idea that the forging of a real-world faith depends upon the ability to see the hidden things within ourselves for what they are and to bring about the process of making necessary changes.

The last two chapters concerning self-exposure noted only the first of a two-part process. They focused on the importance of our dealing with the dark side of the inner self and exposing it to grace.

But the other part of the process of forging a real-world faith is a more positive one, the commitment to regaining what was lost in ourselves when evil disrupted the harmony and order of creation.

If bondage or servitude is the ultimate condition of the spoiled species, liberation or recovery is the condition of someone living a real-world faith. The biblical word used to describe this is *salvation,* a word describing the process by which someone who is lost or in peril is rescued and restored to safety.

Unfortunately, too many people in the community of faith tend to see salvation as a static term, the idea that once one is "saved" there is little else to worry about. But salvation is actually *recovery,* and that is a dynamic word, not a static one.

In biblical times the writers and preachers turned to contemporary situations to form their notions of what it meant to forge a real-world faith. So Jesus would use the word *lost* to describe people in spiritual trouble. *Found* or *saved* was the result when a lost person was brought to safety. *Lost* and *found* came right out of the real world of lost sheep or lost travelers. They were words with which people would have been quite conversant in those days when there were no maps or route signs.

Today the word *recovery* takes on vivid meaning to anyone who suffers with an addiction such as alcohol and is now in the process of pursuing deliverance. And I think that *recovery* describes better what the Bible is talking about when it urges us toward the inner experience of real-world faith.

Probably no modern movement has done more to focus attention on the general idea of recovery than the Alcoholics Anonymous movement and its twelve-step process. By now almost everyone knows that the first step of the twelve calls for an acknowledgment of helplessness (self-exposure), and that one must appeal to a "higher power" for the resolve needed to effect a change.

The Christ-follower, of course, believes in a personal "higher power," the living God, Creator of Heaven and earth. It is not without significance, however, that the human spirit is so constructed that many people have found liberation (temporary or permanent) from some kind of addictive bondage even when the higher power they called upon was something other than the God of Jesus Christ.

Please understand that I am not implying that any old "god" will do. But the fact is that all human beings have been created to believe, to live by faith. And sometimes when the faith "engine" in us is

started up, even though the object of the faith may be misguided, unfocused, or impersonal, amazing things can happen. Again, I hasten to
add that I am not saying this is saving faith. But it does seem as if there
is something we might call healing faith that many people have experienced, although they have never identified it as faith in the God of
Jesus Christ. A Christ-follower always hopes that day will come.

But Alcoholics Anonymous has taught us something helpful to understanding real-world faith. It is not enough simply to engage in the
calling of a "higher power"; one must go beyond the call and enter into
a plan or process of recovery. One must be proactive, doing specific
things that aid in regaining self-mastery. The addict may even tell us
that apart from the positive steps he takes on a daily basis, he has no
self-mastery whatsoever.

Jesus told a story about a man full of demons:

> When an evil spirit comes out of a man, it goes through arid places
> seeking rest and does not find it. Then it says, "I will return to the
> house I left." When it arrives, it finds the house unoccupied,
> swept clean and put in order. Then it goes and takes with it seven
> other spirits more wicked than itself, and they go in and live there.
> And the final condition of that man is worse than the first (Matt.
> 12:43–45).

Jesus' point? Specifically, that when we follow Christ into the inner
life and experience self-exposure, it becomes necessary to replace
the discarded "furniture" or bondage with something spiritually positive and health-giving. If we merely cast things out and take nothing in,
we will likely experience a relapse into bondage or, as the story says, a
revisiting from the evil spirit.

I have been told that recovering alcoholics often go through a renewed battle over addiction about five to seven years after they have
elected to pursue the recovering lifestyle. Many are suddenly tempted
to stop relying on the various steps of recovery such as attending
meetings and making themselves available to fellow alcoholics. They
become strangely confident in their ability to handle what previously
had left them helpless. The sad result is that, not having learned the
lesson the first time, they can fall off the wagon and return to the
former bondage.

As our world becomes more and more aware of the problem of
addiction, which may become, if it isn't already, the great "disease"

of the 1990s, I believe that this parable will ascend to the list of the most frequently related of Jesus' stories.

I first thought of this process as I found myself involved in frequent conversations with young men and women who were trying to overcome addictions not of the chemical kind but more of the spiritual—sexual addiction, greed, and overwhelming experiences of insecurity.

I began to wonder if there wasn't a multistep approach to moving in step with Christ toward increasing self-mastery. It occurred to me that this is a growing issue because so many men and women in the young adult generation have come from families where the principle of self-control or discipline was not learned because there was no opportunity to teach it by example.

Here then are a few ideas about how we follow Christ into the inner space and do some refurnishing.

CHAPTER SIXTEEN

No Vacancy

 A Thought for You, Smithy
Faith grows strongest according to design. Sit quietly sometimes, Smithy; think about where you've come from and where the Master wants you to go with your work. Think about what's going to get you there and what may try to stop you. You have a great future, Smithy, but first you must build it in your heart.

Forging a real-world faith is in part the process of recovering from the effects of what C. S. Lewis called "a spoiled species." But recovery means taking deliberate and disciplined steps to fill the inner life with values, attitudes, and resolves that will penetrate the darkness and replace it with light.

I. The Development of a Life Plan

"We're talking to the bank about money to get this new business off the ground," a couple tells me.

"What confidence do you have that they'll approve your request?" I ask.

"We've got a terrific business plan; it's irresistible."

I look through their plan. It includes the mission of the business: what it's going to accomplish and what the product is all about. It has a description of the resources, both human and capital. It has a definition of a certain market and its potential. And it includes an analysis of the possibilities for sales, revenue, and percentages of profit.

The business plan gives me an idea. *Why not a life-plan?* I wonder to myself. In a world where men and women have seemingly unlimited choices about what to do with their lives, why not a carefully devel-

146

oped life-plan? I quickly learn that it's not a new idea; others have thought about it before me.

"Wait a minute," someone says when I ask aloud the question about a life-plan. "Didn't St. James write somewhere about the dangers of speaking too confidently about where you were going to go one day and where you were going to go the next? Wouldn't he say that a life-plan is a presumptuous affair?"

At first I'm stumped until I reason that James is not against planning; he's against the arrogance of assuming. Even St. Paul was a planner, laying out his strategy for travel and planting churches. Sometimes his plans went awry, and he had to retrace his steps. But at least he had something of a plan that could be modified as unanticipated circumstances arose.

A life-plan. What might it look like? I suggest that it might take up several pages of a looseleaf notebook so that it could be regularly updated as new data and experience are accumulated.

And what would a life-plan accomplish? It would set forth all the possibilities for personal growth and development. It would bring together a statement of all of one's "assets" and "liabilities." Not necessarily the financial kind but the intellectual, emotional, relational, and spiritual kind. The result would be an organized understanding of who I am and where my life might be headed.

A life-plan might consist of the following entries:

1. An immodest listing of a person's significant past experiences (both successes and failures), learning achievements, natural and spiritual gifts and capabilities, key relationships and what they have equipped one to do.

2. An honest assessment of major things yet unlearned, negative tendencies and habits that have to be overcome through discipline, health realities, unresolved relationships where there is bad feeling, and one's present status of relationship with God. What are one's fears, obvious obstacles, and limitations?

3. A status report on one's friends and intimate relationships and what could be done to improve the strength of these. What does one need from them, and what is one prepared to give?

4. A description of the things one likes to do the most in terms of vocation, leisure, service to people, and personal growth. What would one wish to do in the coming years in terms of personal achievements in learning, traveling, making, or creating?

5. A mission statement: a simple sentence or paragraph of what

one has been called by God to accomplish in a lifetime. I'm not speaking only of "full-time Christian ministry." Rather, I'm talking about what a Christ-follower sees as his or her mission through a marketplace experience if that is what God's call is all about.

6. A listing of the things that might be needed to accomplish that goal, such as vocational training, the geographical location in which it might be good to live, the support of family and friends, more education, the acquisition of a mentor, spiritual maturity, and so on.

7. A general projection of vocation. Where is the current career track headed, and where should it go? Are there any possibilities that should be listed? Are there any realistic limits?

8. What financial goals are there? How will these be achieved? And what will be done with the resources when the goals are met?

9. A realistic schedule projecting the step-by-step process by which that mission might be accomplished.

10. If there should be an untimely death, what would one want the family to do in the way of a funeral and the disposition of assets? This is, of course, not a substitute for a will, but including it in a life-plan forces one to think about some things that a lot of us would like to avoid.

It could be said that Jesus had a life-plan, at least a mission statement by which He measured His ministry. A careful reading of Jesus' incarnate life will show that He was not living serendipitously. What He did was according to a prearranged mission. "The Son of Man has come to save that which was lost," He said, reflecting this mission (Matt. 18:11 NKJV). There was life-plan all through His activities.

That mission was at the base of a sorting process by which He chose how to use His time with people. It explains why He would converse with a tax collector who knew He was in trouble and why He would ignore religious leaders who weren't willing to engage in self-exposure. He was "in the business" of intersecting with lost people, not those who arrogantly assumed that they were "found."

II. The Crystallization of Christ-Following Values

When Ray Kroc began to develop the international franchise firm known as McDonald's, he sold his people on three values: quality, service, and cleanliness. Products of the highest possible quality would be sold. The service would be fast and courteous. And the cleanliness of each outlet would be underscored. Kroc knew that the public was tired of undependable food quality, discourteous salespeople, and filthy diners. So he taught a company a new way of thinking and acting. And it worked.

Many of us are now entering into adulthood, but unfortunately we have never really taken stock of the values by which we will chose to live and reflect God's presence in us. One meets professing Christ-followers who are unaware that a hard day's work for an employer is a witness to one's real-world faith. Or that being a thankful person is important when one visits another's home or when one is the recipient of a gift or a favor. Or that dependability, being a person of one's word, is a significant issue in relationships.

At one time, these things were taught in the family context. That can no longer be assumed, so it is a worthwhile exercise for a person who wants to gain self-mastery to ask, What are my top ten values in life? What are the things I will faithfully do that will make life more meaningful to me and to others?

Financial Values

A list of financial values might include things like the proper use of money: choosing to live under my income level and not getting into debt. Paying my bills by a certain time. Putting a ceiling on my lifestyle and not permitting myself to lose touch with the overwhelming majority of people who must live by very basic standards. Being a measurably generous person by setting standards ahead of time concerning the percentage of money I will give away.

Relational Values

A list of relational values might include my standards for interpersonal relationships. Being an appreciative person, taking time to maintain certain personal friendships, relationships with extended family. The desire to be dependable and trustworthy, to commit myself to being a "servant" to people who need what I can give.

Vocational Values

Values can speak to quality of work in my vocation as well as the issue of ethical and moral convictions when it comes to legalities and courtesies. What does a hard day's work mean in my vocational context? What is my responsibility to my employer? To those who work for me? To the customer or client? What does loyalty mean? At what point will my work cease and my attention to other things begin? When is enough, enough?

My wife, Gail, chose for years to make home building her major priority. One of her operating values was the setting of moods through the order in the home, through her emotional leadership, and through her treatment of each family member. We all grew because she pressed this value through everything she did. I know businesspeople who have set a value of always having one young man or woman under their direct mentorship. And I can think of one person who, because of preset values, refused to take another step into further busyness because the limit of involvement had been reached.

Spiritual Values

There must be spiritual values: one's choice to pursue a daily discipline of spiritual development. Bible reading, prayer, study of Christian truth, the priority of worship in the company of others. What does it mean to be a Christlike person? What qualities of personality ought to be enhanced that more vigorously present Christ through a person?

III. Accountability and Inspiration

Self-mastery happens best when we are locked into healthy relationships in which there is a commitment for mutual growth. God made us to be people who can give one another two marvelous gifts: accountability and encouragement.

Accountability is something that some people would like to avoid because it means opening one's inner life up to another and acknowledging what is really there. It means submitting the quality of one's life and certain achievements to the judgment of another. That's a tough way to live, but it brings out the best in us.

For those of us who are married, there is a built-in possibility of sharing the mutual responsibility for growing in those areas we wish to master. Gail and I have been able to pursue a rather vigorous intercessory prayer life during the past few years because we set ourselves to a joint discipline in making it work. We have shared diets together when we felt we needed to lose weight. Daily exercise became a possibility when we did it together. Our reading disciplines, our writing, and our efforts at reaching out to people are things one or both of us might have avoided if we had not had the accountability relationship.

If I were a single person, I would be motivated to develop a friendship with one or more people to provide the same function on a reciprocal basis. I would do my best to help develop a small group of people who took self-mastery seriously and were prepared to help one another toward that objective.

You see accountability at work in Paul's letters to Timothy as the older urges the younger on to a more vigorous ministry at Ephesus. You can see it in Paul's letter to Philemon, a businessman who needed to be motivated to welcome back Onesimus, a runaway slave. Paul makes it very clear that Philemon is going to be held to high standards of performance on what he does, and that Paul is going to visit so that he can know the end of the matter.

We have come through an era of solo achievers in the Christ-following tradition. And a lot of us have learned the hard way that it may produce a few heroes, but it can also produce a bumper crop of losers who find out that much of the development of the practical side of a real-world faith cannot be done alone. Each of us also needs inspiration or encouragement. We need the kind of pep talks that break through the massive amounts of pessimism we are likely to be exposed to every day.

I have come to appreciate the worth of someone who is full of heartening counsel and motivation. The spirited older person who can urge me on; the cheer that comes when Gail and I talk about dreams and possibilities.

I also value the encouragement of a person gifted with enthusiasm. One early morning at one of the lowest points in my life, I turned on the television and saw the face of Robert Schuller. His topic, he said, was enthusiasm.

I found myself anxious to listen. Enthusiasm, Schuller said, was not a circumstance; it was a choice. You choose to be enthusiastic about who you could become and what you might accomplish.

I began to wonder how long it had been since I'd been enthusiastic about anything and quickly realized that it had been far too long. Furthermore, I saw that Gail had been keeping us both going with her enthusiasm. That alone was unfair to our marriage and to God's purposes.

I marched into the room where she was sitting. I was as yet unshaven and not fully dressed. "Listen carefully," I said, "I have decided to become enthusiastic. I've been a drag for too long, and I'm sorry about that. You can count on me to make things happen." Gail was shocked.

And I followed through on my promise as best I could. Morning after morning I arose and resolved to be enthusiastic about everything that was on my plan for the day. And that determination began to alter my perspective on a lot of things about where my life was going.

Dr. Schuller and I are not acquainted, but I have felt indebted to him for that sermon at a time when I needed a positive word so badly. I have heard other kinds of sermons that majored in guilt and pessimism and threatened to cut the heart right out of me. So I know the difference, and I have thus come to appreciate the role of the "inspirer" who can take men and women in the pit of life and lift them out simply by encouraging them to expect better things from the hand of God.

IV. A Vision of the Finish Line

If a person wishes to pursue self-mastery and follow Christ into the inner workings of life, it would be good to engage in one final exercise. Envision the way you want your life to be like in its final decade.

A colleague and I were driving along after having participated in an exciting planning meeting for our church. We came away believing that we might have a plan of activity that would keep us engaged and motivated for years to come. We could not have been more thrilled.

As we drove along, he said, "Do you ever think that we might be living through the most exciting days of our lives right now and that everything from here on out will be downhill compared to this?"

I guess I really hadn't conceived of that possibility then. But I have thought about it now. And I have pledged to myself that that shall not be the case.

When I neared my fiftieth birthday, I sat down with my journal and began to revise my life-plan. I determined that day that I would plan the rest of my life with the assumption that I had thirty years to live. If God sought to interrupt my thirty years with plans of His own, or if He chose to say that I simply didn't have thirty more years, that was OK. But until He said differently, I was going to think in terms of thirty years.

What did I want the last decade of that period to be like? Unfocused? Under control of others? Dominated by leisure? *Or* a time of productivity, alertness, and growth?

I chose the latter without giving the former a serious thought. I wrote in my journal that my goal was to *Finish Strong*. I would not stagger across life's finish line exhausted and relieved that it was over. I would charge the tape with every ounce of energy left within me just as Paul charged the tape when he came to the end of his life in Rome.

To finish strong: growing more, giving more, encouraging more in my seventh decade of life than in my fifth. That vision is an inspiration to me, and it makes my heart pump a bit faster even as I set it on the page. Retire? If retirement means getting out of the way so that younger people can have the power and the chance to engage their creative juices without worrying about me, I plan to retire sooner than most might imagine. But if retirement means to stop thinking, stop growing, stop serving people, stop trying to be an encourager, motivator, or healer, FORGET IT! I'm not retiring. I intend to finish strong.

When I decided that *Finish Strong* was going to be sort of a slogan for the coming decades, I considered whether I knew someone practicing this concept. And immediately I realized that God had given Gail and me a gift in the friendship we have with Dr. and Mrs. Paul Rees.

At the time of this writing, Paul and Edith Rees are in their upper eighties. They are among our closest friends. Paul continues to carry on a vigorous schedule of traveling and speaking. He is a writer, a reader, a thinker, a care-er. He plays golf, advises boards, and loves his wife deeply, but not necessarily in that order. Late in an evening Gail or I will pick up the phone and hear the voices of the Rees on the line asking about our welfare and wondering when we're coming to visit. Finishing strong to me means being like Paul and Edith Rees.

This is the practical side of self-mastery—the proactive rearranging of the inner space so that the clutter and the bondages that can so easily occupy and take over will not have room to stay. When and if the demons in Jesus' story return to the freshly swept house, assuming it is my house, I want them to see the NO VACANCY sign on the front door.

Christ has walked through the interior of my life and asked me to follow Him. I didn't want to do it, but He insisted. And I obeyed. We would forge a real-world faith within. The trip each day is sometimes a painful one, but it means that my real-world faith is being pounded out on the anvil. I like what is coming into shape. Thirty more years, and perhaps self-mastery, along the line that Daniel practiced, will be mine.

THE REAL WORLD
OF THE STREETS

To follow Christ is to make history

in the real world of the streets

and

give Him the gift that involves

the totality of one's life

and that is called kingdom building

CHAPTER SEVENTEEN

Taming the Ferret

A Thought for You, Smithy
Those who forge faith sometimes get burned,
Smithy. To adapt words once spoken by a famous
politician, "If you can't stand the heat, get out of
the forge." As the task gets tougher, other
smithies may drop out, and you'll feel a bit
lonely. Don't even think of joining them.

One Christmas vacation our son, Mark, flew home from college and greeted his mother and me with an unexpected gift, a ferret named Bandit. We swallowed hard and told him we were grateful. A son's arrival at home after three months of absence is not a time for complete frankness.

A ferret, we soon learned, is a cuddly little animal similar to a skunk or maybe a weasel. A young one can also be kittenlike and the source of much enjoyment. We were surprised when Bandit provided us with many humorous moments.

But the enjoyment ceased about four months later. Bandit began to grow up, and we learned the hard way that adult ferrets can become nasty. They may bite, and they may exert independence by neglecting the simple habits of hygiene that everyone, including an animal in a modern home, is expected to observe. The result? A smelly house. And ours was.

All of this caused Gail and me to lose our affection for Bandit and to decide that he had to go. But where? There was no "market" for ferrets that we could discern; no one knocking on the front door of our home to say, "Do you by any chance have a ferret you'd like to sell or give away?"

"Why don't we let Bandit live in the woods up at Peace Ledge?" I

157

asked Gail. It seemed a good idea to me, and I reasoned that there was plenty of forest for him to roam and his personal habits there would not be a problem for anyone.

"I'll talk to the folks at the pet store and see what they think," Gail answered.

"We can't do it," she told me later in the day. The pet store people explained that you mustn't release a tamed ferret (or any tamed animal for that matter) in the woods. It would be dead within twenty-four hours because it wouldn't know how to find its own food and it wouldn't know who its enemies are or how to defend itself against them.

"Funny," I said after Gail explained all of this to me, "Bandit sure knows how to defend himself against me."

We'd tamed Bandit so that he could not survive in his own natural environment. He had become dependent. He could live in the safety and simplicity of our home as long as we would give him free food and drink. But our home was hardly the forest he had been born to inhabit. Obviously, we should have realized that without having to consult with the pet store.

The problems we created for Bandit by taming him have caused me to ask this question about a more important issue concerning real-world faith:

> Are there versions of Christ-following faith that "tame" people in such a way that they find it nearly impossible to cope with the realities of the world in which they work or reside or even play?

This is a tough question, guaranteed to provoke some people to irritation. But no matter what the answer, I believe there is value to it.

The faith Jesus helped His followers to forge was not a taming faith. It certainly readjusted the priorities of a few, in that they left their principal means of income production to preach the gospel, but the majority of Christ-followers remained where they had always been in their communities and in their work. To them, Christ-following meant a new way of living, relating, doing business, and looking at the world and understanding its needs.

Jesus was not interested in putting people into a protected religious cage, as Gail and I had done in caging the ferret. He sent them back to the "forest" (really the streets) where life was tough and survival was always an open question.

"Go! I am sending you out like lambs among wolves," He told seventy-two Christ-followers one day (Luke 10:3). On another day, He said to the inner Twelve, "A student is not above his teacher, nor a servant above his master. It is enough for the student to be like his teacher, and the servant like his master. If the head of the house has been called Beelzebub [or the Devil], how much more the members of his household!" (Matt. 10:24–25).

And then, of course, there was the time when He pointed out that Christ-following had to do with taking up the cross daily. Those are not the words of safety or withdrawal from the affairs of the real world.

A study of the locations where Jesus first called people to faith and taught them how to forge it is instructive. It was not on the campus of a religious institution or in a theological graduate school. Rather, He engaged people in fields, on village streets, out on country roads while traveling, in fishing boats and other working locations, and in the dining room of homes. On the few occasions when He did teach in synagogues, things seemed to end in an uproar caused by people who wanted to play theological games with the Lord.

We have to ask ourselves some basic questions. Where is most faith taught today? In churches. Taught by whom? The ordained clergy. How is faith normally described? In theological language. How is it thought through? In classrooms where people wearing their finest clothes sit in rows or circles and say polite things to one another. And how is the faith illustrated? Against situations arising in the life of the church, rarely outside it. Can this be the best way to forge a faith for the real world? I think not!

A faith forged in the streets is expressed in street language. It is thought through in street forms. It is tested against street situations. And if it is powerful, it changes the people of the streets and probably the streets themselves. And those who say no at least understand what they say no to.

A tame Christ-follower has misunderstood that faith is designed to work best outside the church environment where people work, play, and interact with their friends, working associates, and adversaries. A tame faith causes a Christ-follower to withdraw from conflict, competition, difficult decisions having no simple answer, and involvement with the systems and structures of our social and political systems.

A tame church is one in which the day-to-day matters of the world and its people tend to be ignored in favor of "in-house" subjects. It becomes a place reminiscent of Jonah's "stateroom" on the ship to

Tarsus where he slept the sleep of withdrawal and denial. Out on deck a fierce storm raged; sailors were in mortal danger; and over the horizon, Nineveh, a vast city enmeshed in a value system of cruelty and imperialism terrorized its bordering nations. But Jonah slept through it all in a quiet place until he was rudely awakened. So a tame Christ-follower can "sleep" if he or she is not called to measure faith against the realities of the times outside the cage.

A fresh look at biblical personalities and organizations might suggest that they are anything but tame. Look at the Lord of our faith: Jesus Himself. In Christ-following circles we do not highlight the fact that, before Jesus embarked on His mission as a public teacher, He spent ten to fifteen years making a living doing a job. He was a carpenter, and both His friends and His critics recognized Him as such.

"Is not this the carpenter?" the people of His own community asked when He went public with His teaching. They were used to talking to Him about the things that people talk to carpenters about. So it should not surprise us that they had a bit of a shock when they saw this laboring man suddenly turn to the life of a teacher.

"Is not this the carpenter's son?" another crowd asked.

The point? *Jesus was, first and foremost, a working man from a working man's family. We cannot afford to forget that!*

One does no harm either to the divine nature of Christ or to the Scriptures by musing on a carpenter's way of life. What was the working man's environment like? Did Jesus ever hit His thumb with a hammer or cut Himself with a knife blade? If He did, what did He say in His moment of pain? Were Jesus' products—ox yokes, doors and windows, furniture—competitive in quality and price with those of other carpenters? Did anyone ever complain that His work was substandard and try to return a product? Did He ever haggle over prices for materials at an ancient version of a lumber yard? Did He ever lose out in a bidding competition for a job? And how did He act when fellow carpenters got together and used salty language to complain about prices or government regulations?

Let the mind run on these sorts of questions because they force us to upgrade our view of the incarnate Lord. They help us to see Him in a new light: not as a gentle, somewhat passive, quiet person, but as a tough man, a survivor, one whose resumé of practical experience must have included injuries, the heat of competition, the temptation to cut corners or to use cheap materials while charging for expensive ones. To use the language of the eighties, Jesus was no lightweight.

He wouldn't have survived in the streets if He had been. In fact, the gospel writer notes that He thrived in that world—not the world of theologians and clergy (although He actually did quite well there also), but the world of the people of the street, the tough folks.

Luke observed, "And Jesus grew in wisdom and stature, and in favor with God and men" (2:52). This remark calls to our attention that the Lord was well accepted in His world before He set out on the confrontational ministry of a teacher, which ultimately cost Him His life on the cross. And that acceptance was of a man in the marketplace, doing His work, making His money, and developing a network of relationships. Although some of them apparently went along with the decision, the people of the real world did not put Jesus to death; the people of the religious world made it happen.

Nothing changed when Jesus laid down the hammer and took up the messianic mission. Any man who stands up in a boat in the middle of a storm (much less walks on the water), takes on scores of merchants in the temple grounds, and absorbs the pain of the Roman lash without a whimper is just that: a very tough man. A person who can converse with a Roman centurion on a peer level, successfully challenge a tax collector to clean up his life, and face down the most brilliant minds with their sticky questions has got to be more than adaptable to life in the streets.

We know St. Paul as an apostle. But that was his church identity. I think, when he traveled, the public at large probably knew him first as Paul the tent manufacturer. When he arrived in new communities, did he flash a business card (I am being silly) that said, "The Reverend Paul the Apostle"? Or might it have said, "Paul: Tents and Accessories"?

Why have we never conceived of the times when Paul sat in the marketplace and sold custom-made tents to travelers? Why have we never conjured up the image of Paul driving a hard bargain with wholesalers for the materials used to make a tent: skins, thread, stakes?

Did Paul guarantee his work? Did his tents ever leak? Did anyone ever try to return one of Paul's products? What did the Jew from Tarsus think was a fair markup on his tents? What did he think his work was worth? Did Paul like his work? Did he think that time taken for tent-making was a second-class use of time? Was Paul proud of his products? Did some travelers move about the Mediterranean sleeping in tents with a label somewhere in the seam that said, "Made by Paul of Tarsus"?

I love thinking like this because I realize how long a time I simply carried images of the founders of our faith as nice people in unsoiled clothes who simply talked theology all day long. The fact is that both Jesus and Paul knew the reality of dirty, calloused hands, the conversations of hard-bitten men, and the disappointments of business reversals as well as the satisfaction of a hard-earned sale.

The disciples were not tame either. Peter, James, and John were small businessmen who worked half-naked all night on the lake harvesting fish for a living. Matthew was a tax collector, Simon a political activist. Let me make the point one more time: the followers of the Lord were not passive, withdrawn people who spoke an ethereal religious language. They were people who lived on the cutting edge of their generation, and it was on that cutting edge—not inside a religious perimeter—that they made their faith work. Theirs was a real-world faith.

Consider another question. Why have we too often failed to recognize that right behind the men of the apostolic team were a whole generation of people who lived in homes all of their lives, conceived and raised children, and held down jobs?

Some names? Philemon, mentioned earlier, who apparently hosted Paul in his home at one time or another. He had a large home, a sizable staff, and a successful business of some kind. Onesiphorus, who extended himself to provide encouragement and resources to Paul whenever possible. Lydia, traveling businessperson who apparently thrived as an entrepreneur. The list of specific people is quite long, and some scholars have counted somewhere in the neighborhood of seventy-five names of Christ-followers, most of whom were stay-in-one-place people working in the marketplace to earn their living.

That the New Testament does not recognize these people in greater detail is not surprising because the focus of the compilation of letters and narratives is on the apostolic ventures of a few men who left everything to spread the faith. But they were generally supported, hosted, and encouraged by real-world people who farmed, sold, manufactured, and labored. These people were independent businesspersons, slaves, government employees or contract workers, soldiers, and first-century "professional" people.

It is helpful to go back to the preaching days of John the Baptizer and note his instructions to people who asked him what they were to do to show they were genuinely repentant. At no time is it recorded that he said to quit a job and go into full-time preaching.

Rather, John told tax collectors to return to their tax collecting: an activity we know to be an abominable job with as sleazy a reputation as it was possible to have. And if anyone was hated more than the tax collector (who was usually Jewish), it was the mercenary soldier (who was gentile) who had been shipped in by the Romans from another part of the empire to keep the peace. When soldiers stepped forward and asked about the implications of repentance, John did not suggest that they exit or defect from military life.

To the tax collectors, John's instructions were to collect taxes fairly. It's as if he said, "Someone has to collect taxes; it might as well be a repentant person." And to the mercenaries, his instructions were to not use force to gain from people what the law did not require of them. Again, it's as if John said, "Someone has to enforce the law; it might as well be someone with a repentant mind-set who will do the job with a perspective on justice."

In the Older Testament almost every man and woman did the faith-oriented things for which we credit them *not* in religious environments but in real-world environments. Moses did most of his work in the Pharaoh's conference rooms and in the deserts. Esther did hers in a king's palace. Nehemiah did his on a construction project. These men and women were administrators, scholars, builders, warriors, and merchants. For the most part, they were not clergy. They were the people of the streets, and their faith was defined in terms of a God who wanted to be active in the streets.

Their faith language, recorded in the Bible, was the language of the streets; but we have taken it away from there and made it a religious language. Their jobs were the work of the streets; but we, in our lack of imagination, have taken these men and women off the streets (figuratively speaking) and made them seem like theologians and full-time religious workers. The problems to which they addressed themselves were usually the problems of the streets; but we have taken the problems and spiritualized them.

In short, we have tended to tame these men and women of the Bible, making them smaller than life. It is not that we have not admired them and revered them as heroes. And it is not that we have not wanted to be like them. But it has not occurred to us often enough to wonder if they could have been construction workers on a highway project, manufacturers, franchisees, secretaries, and managers in our day. The result? I'll say it one more time: we do not fully appreciate that their faith was a faith for the real world and not for the restricted environment of professional religion.

Earlier I quoted from Lester and Irene David's biography of Senator Robert Kennedy, a devout Roman Catholic. In another part of their book, the Davids refer to a time during the year after his brother, the president, was assassinated. Kennedy had asked for an interview with his priest, and when they met, he said he had a complaint. The sermons at weekly Mass were too difficult to understand, and his children, whom he regularly took to church, were missing the point.

"My kids are pretty bright," Bobby told [the priest], "and if they don't get [the point], other people won't either." Bobby told the clergyman his sermons should be like his own political speeches, "simple and clear, going directly to the point."

When he realized that he had been, perhaps, too forceful in expressing his opinion, Kennedy backed off.

"I didn't mean to be so intent," he said, "but religion is so important in life. I want my kids to like it. *You all should not be talking about God up there so much. I want to know what God is like down here, how He is concerned with what we do here. I want to know how my life should be lived here now.*" (Emphasis mine)

Even more significant about this conversation was the time in which it took place. As I noted, it happened only a few months after his brother, the president, had been shot. Kennedy was in a state of almost inconsolable mourning and had lost all ability to focus on his sense of direction in life. What should he do now? How should he handle the shock of the grief? Where could he find a new dream?

What Robert Kennedy was saying about his children's need to hear about God in plain talk was really *his* need. He was crying out to hear about a God who was active in the streets—in the real world. And he felt strongly that he wasn't hearing it. Ultimately, he found most of his solace in the works of Albert Camus who had very little to teach him but who was "concerned with what we do here."

In moments of my life when I too was disconsolate in sorrow, I sat in pews of churches listening to hear of a similar God: a God who walked the streets of the real world, not as a tourist but as someone who knew the territory. A God who had something to say about life in the real world: how to survive pain (physical or mental), how to live with the sadness of decisions that have no simple answer, how to find calmness when all about is chaos, how to rid oneself of uncontrollable rage, how to restrain oneself when in the pincers of an addiction or an overwhelming temptation, how to overcome greed, and how to manage ambition. The list is endless.

I found myself listening to hear about a God who provides a ground for hope, who has a plan for cleaning up the messes of this world, who thinks that human life is valuable and worth reclaiming even when it has done its worst to—as some like to say—shoot itself in the foot.

When Christ-following truth is no longer spoken in street language, when it is no longer directed at street life, and when it no longer challenges men and women to live as Christ-followers in those streets, there is no longer a chance for a real-world faith. People are tamed, learning how to act with deftness inside the religious institution. But they do not learn how to live faithfully in the real world.

The result usually plays itself out in one of two ways. Some come to tolerate the outside world; they think of it only in critical terms and use every opportunity to speak ill of it. They withdraw from its needs, refuse to compete in its challenges, and see no responsibility for putting something back into it that might add value.

Others take the second alternative. They inadvertently develop a two-track style of living: one for their Christ-following moments in church or with church people, and one for their times in other settings. We easily call these people hypocrites without asking ourselves in candor, Could it be possible that some double lives are really the fault of the teacher or the preacher who does not understand the real world, and that the people under such influence have no notion or idea of how to apply the teaching to the 95 percent of their week lived beyond the church?

As a young pastor I was filled with explosive vision and a plan for the men and women of my church that, if they had gone along with me, would have filled every waking hour of their week. One day a man in the congregation whom I greatly trusted entered my office (the conversation should have taken place on his turf, not mine) and said, "Pastor, you need to grapple with the fact that lots of us leave here on Sunday and may not even think about the church for several days. We've got jobs and families and lots of problems. And the church doesn't have many answers for some of the things we have to do out there. So you may have to cut some of your plans for us down to size and factor in our need to make livings, raise kids, and generally stay healthy."

The thesaurus built into the memory of my computer offers these parallel words for the word *tame: passive, yielding, acquiescent, compliant, docile, easy, meek, mild, nonresistant, obedient, resigned, submissive, tolerant, unassertive.* Very few of these words would fit the men and women of the Bible pressed into leadership or unique lifestyle by God.

I searched for a word that would be a healthy alternative to the concept of tameness, and it is certainly not *barbarian.* I settled on the word *vigorous* and said to myself, That's what the man or woman of real-world faith looks like. We're talking about a vigorous person who takes the streets of the world by force. And the thesaurus in my computer suggested these parallel words: *effective, forceful, dynamic, energetic, spirited, zesty, peppery* (I especially liked that one), *snappy, compelling, passionate, sturdy.* And I said to myself, I like each of these words. They fit Christ-followers of this age who have made a decision that theirs will be a real-world faith.

I sit at lunch with a man who has spent several years in the New York State prison system for mob-related activities. When he talks, his language and accent are those of the streets. He shares with me the darkness of his past and the price he had to pay for it.

And then he speaks of what it was like to discover the alternative lifestyle of Christ-following. He tells of how he made the choice to change and what difference it made, and then he describes how he's decided to spend the rest of his life challenging other men and women in the prison system to make the same change. His faith is a real-world faith; it is worked out in the visiting rooms, the gangways, and the halfway houses of a prison system. It's a tough life among tough people. He knows firsthand about danger, discouragement, and minimal recognition. But his faith is industrial strength; it's designed for the real world.

A woman gives herself to teaching school in the city. "Why aren't you teaching in the suburbs where the pay and the conditions are better?" I ask.

"I've learned to love city kids," she answers. "They're direct, they're looking for acceptance, and they're willing to work hard if you give them something to care about. I love the challenge. Sometimes I go into that classroom and have to face young men who are much bigger than me physically. One even drew a knife on me once. But it's where I can carry out what God has called me to do." This is real-world faith, and she's making a difference.

In July 1989, a DC-10 carrying almost three hundred passengers and a full crew crash-landed at the airport in Sioux City, Iowa. More than one hundred died; the rest survived. Parts of the rear engine had disintegrated, causing "catastrophic damage" to the plane's hydraulic system and making any normal control of the plane impossible.

The crew members were heroes, the experts said, because they managed to guide the plane through forty minutes of flight to the vicinity of the airport using the increased or decreased thrust of the two remaining engines. No one had ever formally trained for such a procedure; apparently, no one ever thought that what the crew managed to do that day was possible.

When the plane hit the ground just short of the runway at an estimated speed of two hundred miles per hour, it broke into fiery pieces. In one section a woman whom I had known when she was a teenager in our congregation escaped from the burning fuselage with two of her three children. When she realized that the third was not with her, she instinctively returned to the plane. She died of asphyxiation along with that third child when they could not get his seat belt to unlatch.

The people of Sioux City were heroes also. I have read that more than one hundred disaster workers, with only fifteen minutes' notice, were at the airport by the time the plane came to the ground. A physician was already aloft in a helicopter waiting to be airlifted to the site of impact. Sioux City citizens lined up at blood banks to donate blood; others opened their homes to receive survivors. Five times the amount of necessary supplies were shipped to the area hospitals within three hours of the tragedy, and critical medical personnel flooded the trauma centers to provide assistance.

It was a day for heroes. As I saw and read of these events, it occurred to me that I was observing human behavior at its best. *Bursts of beauty,* I came to call them, for there is probably nothing more magnificent in all of creation than a human being giving himself or herself to the need of another. It was not a day for the tame.

The cool, expert competency of a flight crew doing the impossible, the unhesitating courage of a mother returning to the flames for her child, the rallied support of a city—these are the greatest of all beauties. And these bursts of beauty flash like a strobe light in the center of a world we all too frequently think to be darkened with the selfishness of normal human behavior.

As I watched this amazing display of nobility, I wondered if we were not seeing humanity *as it was created to be.* Were we not seeing the motivation, the energy, and the capability that God built into the human breast that were supposed to characterize all of human behavior but all too often are displayed only in moments of great crises or intense competition or in the wake of great insight?

Jesus called upon people to make sure that their noble deeds shone like the glow of a city on a hilltop, not like a strobe that is here for a millisecond and then gone. He called for behavior that would cause the onlooker to say, "The life of God is evident in the activity or character of that person." The Sioux City model of competence, courage, and capacity for heroism was a glimpse, a microcosm, of what God originally made people to be all the time in personal sacrifice and teamwork. Not that every moment is a call to uncommon, life-risking action; rather, the call is to daily, routine nobility of spirit and servanthood. And that is not an environment for tame people.

The Christ-follower believes that one of the greatest bursts of beauty ever known came when our Lord walked unprotestingly to a hill outside Jerusalem and submitted to crucifixion. This One who had known the fatigue, the injuries, and the rough stuff of the carpenter's life, and who had taken on the fiercest critics and the extremities of human need, did the most vigorous thing of all. In atonement for sin, He laid down His life for humanity. He was not tame as I have described tameness. And what He did—giving His life for the thief at His side, the enemy below, and the disheartened friends in the distance (including you and me)—was not an act designed to tame people. It was meant to liberate that nobility once placed in our breasts so that once again it might shine like the strobe and also endure like the glow of the city on the hill.

We could not send Mark's ferret, Bandit, out into the real world. Fortunately, someone came along who loved ferrets (even one that bites and does other mischievous things) and took it off our hands. "We'll give it a good home and lots of love," she said. And so a ferret designed for the vigors of the wilderness went on to live in a safe place where it could be fed and protected.

Men and women who follow Christ should not need spoon-feeding and artificial protection. They should not be tamed. And the fact that too many are being tamed may be one of the great tragedies of our age. We misunderstood the Bible. We tamed those tough folks on those pages in our minds. And all the time, they were tough as nails. I hope they aren't angry with us.

CHAPTER EIGHTEEN

You Can't Go Back to the Island

A Thought for You, Smithy

Smithy, although you need to make a frank assessment of the realities surrounding you, never be cynical or boorishly negative. Always keep in mind what is possible if your faith overcomes the times.

In the first weeks of 1989, Gail and I locked the door of our New Hampshire home in the woods and went to live in the heart of New York City, a move involving contrasts of environment something akin to going from the North Polar cap to the tropics.

A congregation, made up of people almost all younger than we are, asked if I would be their pastor. When I accepted their invitation, they leased an apartment for us, and we joined them and the millions of human beings who make up one of the world's great cities.

The sixty-year-old church building where I preach on most Sundays is located on Manhattan's East Side. The less-than-one-year-old apartment, located on Roosevelt Island in the middle of the East River, is only minutes away.

Each morning when I head for my office, I ride a Swiss-built tramway over the river from the island to Second Avenue and Sixtieth Street. If I make the trip during what is called rush hour, the tram cabin may be filled with more than a hundred people. I have come to know more than a few of them, if not by name, then by sight and friendly greeting. If the tram were to be dismantled and replaced by a subway under the river, many islanders would grieve the loss because

169

the tram ride can be as much a social event as it is a practical means of commutation.

The tram provides a spectacular four-minute ride; its cable way parallels the Queensboro Bridge. Riders see the United Nations Building immediately to the south, the Empire State Building to the west, and the pencil-like skyscraper apartments rising like a wall along the river to the north. If the tram ride begins from the Roosevelt Island end, there is relative quiet in the cabin unlike that soon-to-be-opened subway below the ground whose clamor numbs the ears. The only sound over the river is the low-volume talking of the passengers.

When the tram nears its terminus point in Manhattan, however, the ceaseless racket of the city becomes more apparent. As the din intensifies, you can sense a rise in tension as tram passengers brace themselves in preparation for another day in the place affectionately known as the Big Apple.

A violent rainstorm was in progress one recent morning when I boarded the 6:30 A.M. tram. As each passenger entered through the doors, he collapsed his dripping umbrella and stood in silence, perhaps not knowing whether to complain about the rain or give thanks for it since New Yorkers were aware of a pending drought emergency.

When the doors closed, the tram silently nosed its way up the cable track and was soon dangling high above the East River. The gusty wind blew the cabin back and forth so much that I quipped to the person next to me that it might be time to pass out airsick bags. But either he didn't understand me, or he didn't think my comment was funny because he didn't respond. With each minute the rain seemed to beat down harder; a thick fog engulfed the buildings we usually saw. There was nothing laudable about the view *or* the ride that day. Smart people would have stayed home.

Then as we neared the end of the ride and descended toward the "dock" on the other side of Second Avenue, we heard the familiar sounds of Manhattan; but this time the noise rose up in a fury that seemed unprecedented. As we descended above Second Avenue we could see that it was like a parking lot of jammed vehicles from Eightieth Street to the north and to Forty-second Street to the south. Every driver, it seemed, was choosing to vent his frustration by leaning on his automobile horn. Everything—the rain and wind, the confusion of the traffic below, and the earsplitting noise—was deafening, intimidating, a portent of the day we were about to face. In a word, it was ghastly; and one felt like we were being slowly lowered into a boiling cauldron of human madness. Someone muttered aloud, "This is insane; I wonder if they could turn this sucker around and take us back to the island."

I turned and caught the eye of the attendant who pushed the buttons to make the tram go and stop. He was about to remind passengers over the loudspeaker to hold on as the tram "docked." He usually added to the end of his daily instructions a friendly "have a nice day."

"Jimmy," I asked with a grin, "are you seriously contemplating telling us to have a nice day today?" My question caused him to take a reflective look out the window of the cabin, note once more the turbulent weather and the mindless chaos below, and test it all against that phrase with which he routinely dismissed us from the tram.

Then after a second or two, he brightened and said to me and the other passengers, his English marked with a delightful Hispanic accent, "Well then, today, everybody just do the best that you can."

The people in the tram cabin convulsed with laughter. The tram conductor was aware of exactly what we were facing, and his challenge fit the situation. Life was going to be rugged in New York that day from the moment we hit the wet, noisy streets, and it was ridiculous to think anything different.

Whoever wanted to turn around and go back to the island had a great idea. But life with its responsibilities isn't like that. One has to get on with business, whatever that may be and whatever the circumstances; one has to take the measure of the day and "just do the best that you can." No employer would accept a phone call saying, "I went back to the island today; the hassle on Second Avenue was too great."

A real-world faith has to be able to function under circumstances like that. In fact, it may even relish the opportunity. Real-world faith does not retreat from the havoc of places like Second Avenue. It engages; it challenges; it provokes. It heads for the difficult addresses and dares to be tested. It does not demand an early return to the tranquillity of the island, wherever that may be for each of us; it does not seek a premature return to the church to hide in the relative benignity of religious programs.

An aeronautical engineer invites me to visit his research laboratory and introduces me to the fascinations of a wind tunnel where he and his colleagues test the configurations of various designs for new aircraft. At one end of the tunnel, powerful bursts of air are generated that flow across the surfaces of a model.

The real test of an airplane, however, is not in the wind tunnel; it is in the air above the surface of the earth. Until that model is turned into an actual airplane and flown into the air, we do not know how reliable it really is.

Too much faith is tested in a kind of wind tunnel—under safe and predictable conditions. Real-world faith is tested in the streets where real people pose real challenges for choices and deeds.

Real-world faith gets its shape from the lessons learned on occasions such as the day I previously mentioned when Peter, James, and John stood on a mountaintop with Jesus and shared a glorious experience with Heavenly visitors. When it was over, Peter had an idea. "Let's pitch some tents here," he said, apparently hoping they could extend their visit. We can assume that it was a nice day and that the view and the company were unsurpassed.

But that was not to be. No tents, no buildings, no shrines, Jesus said. Only movement: back to the valley. A demon-possessed child with a desperate father awaited their descent. And beyond that, an appointment with a cross in Jerusalem many miles to the south.

It's a story with powerful implications: that description of events on the mountain. Like so many of us might have, Peter wanted to hang out, as New Yorkers put it; that was convenient and desirable. Jesus, on the other hand, could have stepped off the mountain in the company of Moses and Elijah and returned to Heaven; that would have been His right. But real-world faith does not listen to either convenience or rights; it heads impatiently for the action. And Jesus led the way.

The valley below was indeed like Second Avenue. It reeked of all the unpleasant things of life. Really, why go there? Christian theology has long taught that the heart of a human being is *not* a nice place and that the "Second Avenues" of the world are not always nice places either. That does not mean the world is not beautiful in terms of its scenery (where we have not polluted and stripmined), its art, and its occasional efforts of goodness.

But by and large, it does mean that we must look at the world along the lines of what I and my fellow commuters saw that day as the tram lowered us into the chaos of the city. The world is touched, polluted, by the power of evil, and that has been the baseline of history ever since the first generation of human beings thumbed their noses at God.

I would never want to ignore the fact that there are great numbers of good people, beautiful places, and remarkable achievements in each generation. And they pack a powerful wallop. But we stand on safe ground if we realize that there is a general instability of spirit and that things that seem genuinely good can turn sour or ugly overnight.

Jesus was blunt about the harshness of the real world when He said to the disciples, "The world will make you suffer. But be brave. I have defeated the world." Note that He did not say, "Have a swell day!"

Mine is a gloomy assessment, but it is a real one. Humanity has at best a grade of C– in policing itself. And for every good moment when some person or some group steps out in a noble effort, there are probably five other examples of exploitation, greed, cruelty, injustice, or insensitivity. How does anyone really know what is an accurate ratio? We are left at best to the mercy of sheer guessing. But it is safe to say that a global view of humanity's status will not provide an optimistic picture.

So where does that leave us in our forging of a real-world faith? It leaves us with this challenge:

Shape a faith that looks the day squarely in the face, accepting what *is* rather than what we wish might be. *Develop* a faith that is "plug compatible" with the issues, the language, the wounds, and the conspiracies of our time. *Present* a faith capable of pressing God's light into darkened situations.

To repeat the lesson of my tramway metaphor: the Christ-follower may want to return to the island, but he cannot. A large part of life is in the "city" (wherever that is for each of us) with its noise, its business, its people. So what does it mean to do the best that you can?

We've had enough statistics describing the sadness of our world. Everyone who wishes to know has access to the growing numbers of poor and homeless, the swelling populations of prisoners and political refugees. We know all we need to know about AIDS, poverty, slums, illiteracy, violence, and abuse if knowledge alone could impel us to remedial action. We know in round numbers how many people have never heard the Christian gospel and how many places have no church. If we do not act to alleviate these tragic conditions that dehumanize increasing numbers of human beings and blight our world, it is not because we do not know something specific and measurable about them.

But perhaps we need to take another kind of look—beyond the

statistics—at this real world on "Second Avenue." We need to take a look that is a bit more intuitive or subjective. Let me advance some simple statements that the Christ-follower must take into account as he asks the question, What will I encounter, what will I do, and what should I be on "Second Avenue"?

Life Is Difficult

Scott Peck said it that way first when he wrote his book *The Road Less Traveled*. It seemed such a simple statement when I first read it. But profound thoughts are often simply put, and Peck's three little words are a great example of that.

Life is indeed difficult. It is difficult because the influences or forces breaking in upon a man or a woman like the relentless waves of the ocean are often unpredictable and barely controllable.

Some people insist that life isn't supposed to be difficult and that struggle isn't supposed to happen. Thus, when the difficulties show themselves, these people are surprised and not a little angry. They assume that what they are experiencing is an exception when, in actuality, they are experiencing the rule.

A whole generation of young people somehow seem to have developed the notion that careers ought to begin with a bang and that a person ought to be earning in six figures of American dollars before the age of thirty. The October 1987 crash of the stock market sent many in that generation into shock, and more than a few discovered for the first time in their lives that there could be downsides to every upward trend. They found out that life can be difficult.

I have stood with a farmer and watched silently with him as a hail storm has swept across his land, wiping out his entire wheat crop but leaving the neighbor's crop untouched just a few hundred feet across a section road. The sadness of the loss is compounded by the bewildering discrimination in the storm's "decision" to create a winner and a loser. Out in that field I discovered that life is difficult.

I have sat with a young father of three children while he was informed by the physician that his wife who had just sustained a cerebral hemorrhage would not last the night. In that waiting room I found out that life is difficult.

I have listened to parents weep as they returned from the court where their son had been sentenced to prison for dealing in drugs. And it has been evident as I have shared in their anguish that life is difficult.

I have been acquainted with a man who is quadriplegic. Every hour of his waking life must be spent in a wheelchair, and every effort to do something for himself is laborious. In getting to know him, I have learned that life is difficult.

Real-world faith assumes the difficulty of life, and it learns not to complain. It understands the meanness of evil and grieves its existence but anticipates its demise. It hears the words of Jesus: "In the world you will have tribulation; but be of good cheer, I have overcome the world" (John 16:33 NKJV).

Life Is Unfair

If the fact of difficulty in life is clear to see, the *why* behind the difficulty presents more of a challenge to our human understanding. We have no trouble coming to terms with a difficulty *if* what caused it is obvious.

A person chooses to cheat on his income tax, and we understand why, when he is caught, he loses everything. That's fair. A teenager drinks too much and loses his life in a car crash. The cause of the tragedy is clear, and although we are grieved at the loss of life, we know that this happened because a person chose to flaunt the rules concerning driving under the influence. Harsh, but that's fair too. And we understand when a businessperson bets his fortune on a deal that falls through because there is a sudden downturn in the economy. We feel badly for him, but we are not confused as to the reasons for what has happened. It's a fair risk.

But more often than not, the answers to the *why* of the difficulty are not so obvious. In the midst of difficulty, we are tempted on many occasions to cry out, THIS IS UNFAIR! Why do the good die young? Why are the crooked sometimes more prosperous than the straight? And why does the prankster get caught while the gangster gets off? We want to cry foul to someone who is responsible. We seek an appeals court that could provide a hearing when we are dissatisfied with the outcome of certain events. We want to demand of God that every circumstance be evaluated in something called fairness, and by that, we mean that good actions should mean good consequences and good people should inherit good rewards. We want to know the whole story so that if God needs to be second-guessed, we can do it.

That's something of what Job in the Older Testament had in mind. When his life filled up with great loss, he demanded a hearing from God:

O, that I had someone to hear me!
I sign now my defense—let the
    Almighty answer me;
let my accuser put his indictment in writing (41:35).

But Job didn't know the whole story. He didn't know that his life was a proving ground for faithfulness. And as far as we can see, even at the end of the book, there is no indication that God informed Job as to the story behind what had happened to him. We are left to infer that explanations would come later.

Real-world faith understands that "we see through a glass darkly" to use words written by St. Paul. Man's limitations make most of the thoughts of God inaccessible to him. Real-world faith realizes that un-fairness (if that is what it actually is) is one more attribute of a system run amok with evil. Further, real-world faith looks in hope to a day when we shall sit in the presence of God and hear the unexplainable explained.

Life Is Sad

If we remove the blinders from our eyes and take a hard look at the real world, we'll have to conclude that happiness—much of which is really an illusion or a momentary bubble—is really in short supply. An overwhelming majority of human beings simply do not live happy lives.

Walk the streets of the world's great cities; visit the countries of the African deserts where people are starving; and read about life in the totalitarian states. Life in these places where the majority of humanity lives is filled with sadness. Most people in our world do not think in terms of vacations, bonuses, and cellular telephones. Rather, their thinking centers on matters of survival: food, shelter, and protec-tion. As some have noted, we in the Western world live on an island of affluence in a sea of poverty.

I saw sadness a few years ago on a chilly morning when I walked across a field in the Ethiopian countryside where several thousand people had come during the night, hoping to find food at a feeding center. Having only the clothes on their backs, most of them had slept through what was left of the night on ground absolutely bereft of vege-tation. As I made my way through the crowd, several dozen children crowded about me. Those closest grabbed my hands; others put their arms about my legs and waist. I commented to a doctor who accompanied me, "These are some of the most affectionate children I have ever seen."

"It's not affection they're seeking," he said. "They want your body warmth. They're freezing, and it's all the worse because they're so hungry."

That day I learned that life can be very, very sad. I cried.

A less discernible but just as real sadness lies barely under the surface of a significant percentage of the world's affluent people. It's sadness disguised beneath the surface of stretch limos, condominiums, Club Med travel packages, cocktail parties, and designer clothes. But what lies beneath that surface? Fear of things like being used, growing old, losing control of life and health, being left alone, forfeiting hard-earned status, and (worst of all) dying. It's a more sophisticated sadness, and it only fully announces itself when one comes off the last high. But it is very real and not too difficult to bring to the surface.

In Tom Wolfe's novel *The Bonfire of the Vanities,* one of the leading characters, Sherman McCoy, a successful bond broker on Wall Street (Wolfe calls him the Master of the Universe and in so doing dabbles in a bit of his own theology), finds his life as a professional man, as a socialite, and as a person of acknowledged wealth in a state of disintegration when he is accused of a hit-and-run accident.

As he muses upon the friends and associates who have deserted him in his hour of public exposure, he says to his lawyer,

It's . . . sobering how fast it goes when it goes . . . all these ties you have, all these people you went to school with and to college, the people who are in your clubs, the people you go out to dinner with—it's all a thread . . . all these ties that make up your life, and when it breaks . . . that's it . . . that's it.

It would be nice to assume that happiness is the norm of human experience; it isn't. No matter how many media presentations try to suggest that a problem-free life is possible, the evidence points in the other direction.

A real-world faith does not try to pretend that sadness doesn't exist. It believes in relieving the effects of sadness whenever possible. It is not tricked into believing that happiness is the lot of everyone who claims happiness. It is not seduced with promises of permanent relief from sadness when it knows that until Christ comes to make all things new, sadness will be a predominant feeling for a huge segment of humanity. Then, and only then, does real-world faith expect to see all sadness obliterated. It rejoices in John's words of that time when "there will be no more death or mourning or crying or pain" (Rev. 21:4).

Jesus understood sadness wherever He went. He cried in anguish at the grave of his friend, Lazarus. He expressed great sorrow over those who refused to see their need for self-exposure and repentance; He actually wept over the arrogance of Jerusalem as He predicted its coming destruction. This is not to paint a picture of a gloomy Jesus. It's simply to recognize that He saw the disparity between what actually was and what He knew things could have been. And it left Him deeply remorseful.

Life Is Complex

Other lamentable affirmations need to be recognized as characterizing our real world. Life is complex. Its bits and pieces do not flow toward a common goal like the various tributaries of a great river; rather, its bits and pieces tend to diverge like the branches of a great tree.

Life Is Also Unsafe

Life is also unsafe. There are serious consequences and circumstances, the volume of which we can only estimate. We are all but an instant away from death or disaster, and those of us who live in the affluent Western world have no idea how artificial is our safety. We are the tiny minority of the world that does not live in constant fear and caution—whether it be safe water to drink, vulnerability to bandits, or susceptibility to disease.

Life Is Mostly Routine

Life is also mostly routine. It is made up of a concert of events that have to be repeated again and again. Boredom is a state of mind only conjured up by those who think that life ought to offer them an unending series of excitements. There is a great temptation to describe our lives according to our infrequent high points rather than to recognize that the large part of our existence is made up of the plodding of the sleep-eat-work-relate cycle. We have to live with this fact.

Life Is Unraveling

Finally, let me add one more melancholy observation. Life is in the process of unraveling. A civilization is in a state of decline. The consequences of years of thoughtless stewardship of our resources are coming upon us. The results of the breakdown of the family are now being felt in one country after another. And the dissolution of mutual values continues at an increasing pace.

In the movie *Wall Street* there is a tense scene in which Gordon Gekko, the company takeover expert, gives a speech to the stockholders of Teldar Paper. He is trying to convince them that it is in their financial interest to vote his way and to repudiate the present management of the company. As he concludes his appeal he says,

> The point is, ladies and gentlemen, that greed, for lack of a better word, is good. Greed is right; greed works. Greed clarifies, cuts through, and captures the essence of evolutionary spirit. Greed in all of its forms: greed for life, for money, for love, knowledge, has marked the upward surge of mankind, and greed, you mark my words, will not only save Teldar Paper but that other malfunctioning corporation called the USA. Thank you very much.

I am told that these words spoken by Michael Douglas (who played Gekko) were lifted from the speech of a well-known Wall Street businessman who is presently in prison for doing, "for lack of a better word," greedy things.

This is the real world, the "Second Avenue" into which we are lowered each day. For some, that real world will be at home with one or more small children, and there will be the challenge of facing all the nitty-gritty details of child-discipleship and home development. For others, the real world will be the campus where ideas are the order of the day, some of them not particularly friendly to faith. But for the large majority, "Second Avenue" will be the marketplace where one's labor is converted into income.

You have three alternatives when you face this real world: you can go back to the island where it's safe, you can do the best that you can and let the results take care of themselves, or you can determine that you have a mission as a Christ-follower to make a difference on Second Avenue and reclaim a piece of it in the name of Jesus. At least the piece where you're standing.

Real-world faith does not go back. It advances. And wherever it goes, a part of the world knows that God's presence has been there. Jesus had some of these thoughts in mind when He took His followers aside and told them He was going to send them out to help others forge a real-world faith. He did not make the prospects of a good day sound too bright:

> I am sending you out like sheep among wolves. Therefore be as shrewd as snakes and as innocent as doves. Be on your guard against men; they will hand you over to the local councils and flog you in their synagogues. On my account you will be brought before governors and kings. . . . But when they arrest you, do not worry about what to say or how to say it. At that time you will be given what to say, for it will not be you speaking, but the Spirit of your Father speaking through you.
>
> Brother will betray brother to death, and a father his child; children will rebel against their parents and have them put to death. All men will hate you because of me, but he who stands firm to the end will be saved (Matt. 10:16–22).

He or she who has met God in the Heavenlies as Christ's guest, who has engaged in self-mastery by following the Lord into the inner space, will face this challenge also—and will face it with anticipation and joy. The power will be there when needed.

CHAPTER NINETEEN

Weekdays in the Real World

A Thought for You, Smithy
The kind of faith you say you want to shape,
Smithy, doesn't happen overnight. Every effort at
the forge counts for something. When it comes
time to present your work to the One who called
you, you want to be able to present Him with ex-
actly what He asked for.

Out of the stories of the workplace comes the anecdote of a young person who applied for a job and presented recommendations from a pastor and a Sunday school teacher. After he had studied the papers, the manager said, "I'm impressed with the nice things these people have said about you. It's obvious that you appear to them to be just what we need. But I would very much like a recommendation from someone who is acquainted with your activities on the weekdays."

If there has been a "star" in this book, it has been Daniel of the Older Testament. Daniel, the man of real-world faith, in a place like Babylon—the epitome of pagan power and hedonism. It should be a point of encouragement to us that Daniel made a useful contribution to his generation *on the weekdays in the streets* where the drama of life took place. The model for this book has not been a clergyman or a full-time Christian worker. It has been a layman who had a job in which he was surrounded by the same kind of people we meet in the market-place every day. I say the obvious only because I want to keep emphasizing that real-world faith is exercised mostly on the weekdays in the hours when people are in their homes, at work, on the campus, or at play.

I have a continuing curiosity about how people do their work on those weekdays. As a pastor, I know what they look like on Sunday morning when they enter the world of weekend church. Most of them wear suits or dresses; most of them do whatever the program or the service bulletin tells them to do; and most of them smile a lot and say nice things.

Of course, some character traits and skills similar to weekday activity show in the few who make weekend church life happen. Ushers can be leaders; Sunday school teachers, communicators; and trustees, administrators. But in most cases we have little knowledge of how each of us lives the rest of the week. Weekend church is hardly an accurate indicator of what a Christ-follower really is in terms of character and contribution.

My first pastoral experience out in farm and ranch country was unique. On Sunday we worshiped, but on the weekdays we headed for the fields. I wasn't there every day, but I saw enough when I occasionally joined the men and women of the community herding cattle, harvesting wheat, and stacking hay bales. I came to know the working character of the men and women of the congregation. I knew those who were lazy, sloppy, grumbling, or pessimistic. And I saw those who were honest, faithful, hard-working, and quick to help.

But when I moved to the suburbs, I knew almost nothing about the weekdays of people unless I paid visits to a job site or to a home. But even then what I saw was under somewhat controlled conditions and could easily be misrepresented.

I saw how easy it is to be two different people on weekends and weekdays when I was in traffic one afternoon. The driver of another car, upset with something I'd done, blew his horn, screamed at me through the windshield, and underscored his thoughts with an obscene gesture. A second later, he recognized that it was his pastor with whom he was communicating. He was the same man who the previous Sunday had vigorously shaken my hand at the door and assured me concerning the powerful blessing of the sermon. On Sunday, a warm hand; on the weekday, a hand gesture.

It would be helpful if we could sit down with Daniel's boss (in his case, several kings) and ask what it was like to have this man around on weekdays. What qualities of character and what work habits did he consistently exhibit? Such an interview might go some distance in helping me to understand how real-world faith is "fleshed out" when people head for the marketplace.

But the interview technique is obviously impossible. And so the next best thing is another run-through of his biography, this time looking for overarching principles or operating values that marked Daniel's work style. I found eight, which I decided to call *weekday kingdom qualities*. There are probably many others, but here are a few worth our meditation.

1. A Kingdom Perspective

Daniel always knew who was in charge.

At least three times Daniel made it clear that he knew who was Master of the universe. And it wasn't any of the Babylonian or Persian kings. Daniel came to Babylon as a young man with an unalterable awareness of the One he was working for: the God of his fathers, the Lord of Israel. While he turned in a full day's work for the king in the Babylonian court, his efforts were pegged against the pleasure of his God. Fortunately, for the kings Daniel served, this meant that they doubtless gained more out of Daniel than anyone else on the payroll.

Because Daniel had a kingdom perspective, he refused to permit any of the kings to dominate his spirit. His prayers and his direct comments to the kings show exactly how he felt about their power. To Nebuchadnezzar, he made it plain that the Babylonian Empire and the present regime in particular held sway in the world only because the God of Heaven had willed it so: "You, O king, are the king of kings. The God of heaven has given you dominion and power and might and glory; in your hands he has placed mankind and the beasts of the field and the birds of the air. Wherever they live, he has made you ruler over them" (Dan. 2:37–38).

Later he would warn this same king that his authority might be suspended for a time: "[This message] means that your kingdom will be restored to you *when you acknowledge that Heaven rules*" (Dan. 4:26, emphasis mine).

To Belshazzar, he said, "You praised the gods of silver and gold, of bronze, iron, wood and stone, which cannot see or hear or understand. But you did not honor God who holds in his hand your life and all your ways" (Dan. 5:23).

Daniel made these blunt, confrontational statements to kings who could have annihilated him on the spot. But he never flinched and never soft-pedaled his words because he kept his eye on the God high above their thrones who made them look, by contrast, rather puny.

Daniel teaches this: on weekdays, the person of real-world faith gauges every activity not against the opinions of people but against those of God. And when moments of divergent opinion occur, one is careful to remember where the real power lies.

2. Prudent Flexibility

Daniel knew when to back off and when to fight with bare knuckles.

This working principle is more inferred than specifically documented. But as one reads and rereads the weekday life of Daniel, it is apparent that he made an uneasy peace with the "system" in which he had to work. Daniel lived, as I have noted before, with a lot of "gray" issues: decisions and choices that didn't always please him. Surely there were times when his spirit was greatly offended at pagan ways, and he had to swallow hard. But if he was going to play an influential role in the life of the kings on those greater occasions when Heaven's voice had to be strongly represented, he had to be flexible.

We have an indication of the kind of brutal world in which Daniel lived when we read the story of the lions' den. When Daniel was liberated following a restful night with the lions, his accusers *and their families* were brought to the same site and thrown in the same den. There is no indication that Daniel intervened in this matter and suggested grace. I would like to think I would have. But that is not the way things were done where Daniel lived.

Daniel's presumed flexibility could be a topic of great controversy among Christ-followers. One might legitimately ask, How far can one compromise convictions? How many times can one close one's eyes to injustices, illegalities, insensitivities before one has to separate from the system creating them? Daniel gives us no simple answer to the question—only his own actions. And we learn that Daniel remained when others might have disappeared, but he was there to ram home his convictions when major policy issues could be influenced.

When Nebuchadnezzar was told to "renounce your sins by doing what is right, and your wickedness by being kind to the oppressed," the words came from an insider, Daniel, who had proved himself worthy to be heard (Dan. 4:27).

3. Communication Based on Wisdom and Tact

Daniel communicated with people out of a wellspring of extraordinary insight.

"Daniel spoke to [Arioch] with wisdom and tact," we are told in the account of the crisis concerning Nebuchadnezzar's bothersome dream (Dan. 2:14). Wisdom and tact: interesting that the two are linked together. A person with wisdom and no tact or a person with tact and no wisdom is hard to imagine, but either one would be relatively useless in a key moment in a business or a government.

Daniel's wisdom was an admirable quality that every Christ-follower might seek to acquire. The word describes one's ability to blend raw knowledge with an awareness of God's overarching purposes. Wisdom is the greater sense of how things are supposed to be. Solomon prayed for it and received it. Daniel had it and used it.

The world then and now has plenty of bright people, and on most weekdays, the bright people make a lot of things happen. But bright people have limits, and that was the situation on the morning after Nebuchadnezzar's dream. The smart folk couldn't fathom what to do. Only the wise man, who had a hand on the deeper things, was able to come to the rescue.

On the other hand, tact is the capacity to communicate what wisdom produces. The word indicates that when Daniel presented his plan to Arioch for dream-interpretation, he did it with words and concepts fully comprehensible in that culture. Daniel was believable.

If the world is not overpopulated with wise people, it may not be inundated with tactful people either. Many of us are good with words and persuasion. We understand the value of meeting at power lunches, wearing authoritative clothing, and choosing the chair of influence at the conference table. We have learned the preferred ways to "close" a sales presentation, how to use a special joke at the beginning of a speech, and how to present facts with computer-generated graphics. But tact represents a greater ability: to command the attention of another's heart and to raise within another a certainty that one has sensible answers.

When the Christ-follower enters the real world to practice faith on the weekday, he must go with the prayer that he carries wisdom and tact with him. This must be the goal of the secretary who assists an executive and has to deal in utter frankness; it must be the goal of the manager who must inspire and motivate; and it must be the goal of the engineer who must build a team in order to get a product out the door.

4. Humility

Daniel never advertised or sold himself.

On those occasions when Daniel conferred with his superior, he had opportunity to engage in self-aggrandizement. He had solutions no one else produced. He had information no one else provided. He had capacities no one else possessed. These were gifts from God, and Daniel knew it.

Because they were gifts, Daniel never attempted to profit from them in terms of advancing himself or gaining further wealth. When kings attempted to praise him for his abilities, he quickly diverted the glory away from himself, insisting that this was merely the life of God in him.

To be sure, the woman or man in the marketplace or the community today cannot easily respond to a "one-minute praise" by saying, "The honor you're giving me belongs to the Lord." Nor can one say in a typical resume of an achievement or a skill that the previous successes have come from God.

Nevertheless, Christ-followers ought to carefully cultivate a quality of humility that resists the need to pursue profit and credit for every accomplishment. When may it be proper to promote ourselves or our capacities? The key test is simple. What is this doing to our souls? Is the praise, self-induced or given by others, deserved, and does it represent what we truly are in the eyes of the Lord of the kingdom?

Inside the Christian perimeter, a distressing tendency combats the spirit of Daniel-like humility. All the techniques of public relations and advertising have been brought to bear to "hype" preachers, organizational leaders, authors, and unusual kingdom achievers. People like myself who have the privilege of giving public talks are often tested when introduced at a meeting or a dinner. The superlatives of the emcee can be intoxicating, actually injurious to the soul. And one understands why Daniel wouldn't accept adulation that did not belong to him.

5. Intelligence

Daniel was smart!

To [Daniel] God gave knowledge and understanding of all kinds of literature and learning. And Daniel could understand visions and dreams of all kinds. . . . The king talked with [Daniel] and he found none equal to [him]; so [he] entered the king's service. In every matter of wisdom and understanding about which the king questioned [him], he found [him] ten times better than all the magicians and enchanters in his whole kingdom (Dan. 1:17–20).

We are left to our imagination to understand the full implication of these comments. The emphasis is on what God did in giving Daniel (and his colleagues) knowledge and understanding. But we know enough about life to realize that this extraordinary mental capacity did not come like a sudden transfusion or like an off-the-shelf computer program. It came through hard work and study. One can assume that Daniel took his brain seriously and conditioned it as an athlete would his body.

Daniel was a thinker, and he inspires me to this great exercise of the brain, which is not encouraged enough in Christ-following circles. None of us are helped in the forging of a real-world faith when our preaching and teaching about following Christ is reduced to rules and rigid systems that seem to make it unnecessary to think. If life is complex, the thinker whose brain is networked with the mind of God is going to know how to make sound decisions with discernment in the real world.

6. Integrity

Daniel could be trusted with the cash box.

It pleased Darius to appoint 120 satraps to rule throughout the kingdom, with three administrators over them, one of whom was Daniel. The satraps were made accountable to them so that the king might not suffer loss. Now Daniel so distinguished himself among the administrators and the satraps by his exceptional qualities that the king planned to set him over the whole kingdom (Dan. 6:1–3).

Human nature hasn't changed much in several thousand years, and it is likely that the kings of Babylon had the same problem that governments are having today: people trying to stuff their pockets with a little extra.

In an empire as big as Babylon's, the control of the king's business had to be an enormous undertaking. Whom do you trust with the revenue? How do you make sure that the laws are being kept? To whom do you turn to guarantee the structure is going to accomplish what it's been designed to do? Where do you find a person whose word is his bond, who won't sell out the first time someone comes along with a better offer? Who? People like Daniel.

A real-world faith includes integrity in its list. Many of us appreciate this quality because we have seen the seeds of weakness in our own spirits. And having known at one time or another the pain that a lack of integrity causes, we have grown to appreciate how imperative this quality really is.

One grows troubled about the number of times people in business complain that working with Christians can be an unhappy experience: bills not paid, promises not kept, a day's labor not fully given, or work not guaranteed.

On the other hand, there is this man, Daniel, who made himself indispensable to all he worked for. They could count on his word. They were looking for an integral man, and they found him. Can he be found today?

When Daniel's enemies decided that he had too much power and that he had to go, they started by investigating every inch of his life to find a point of vulnerability. They found nothing.

As I read of their efforts, I am reminded of the vigor with which the press often goes after a candidate who declares his intentions to run for public office. An investigative reporter uncovers an episode of cheating on an examination thirty years earlier or an illegal exchange of favors that seemed of little consequence fifteen years ago. Nothing a person does anymore seems immune to a probing reporter. Did Daniel go through this sort of inquiry? Apparently.

Again, his enemies found nothing: "They could find no corruption in him, because he was trustworthy and neither corrupt nor negligent. Finally these men said, 'We will never find any basis for charges against this man Daniel unless it has something to do with the law of his God'" (Dan. 6:4–5).

And that's when they came up with the law about prayer and its mandatory sentence to be thrown in the lions' den. But after an initial victory, they lost everything. Ultimately, you can't beat a person of integrity.

7. Leadership Skill

Daniel was influential.

Daniel's capacity to administer programs was obvious. Each time this came to the attention of a new king, he ended up in charge of something. But his leadership was more than management skill. It was his ability to influence people, to make them think, and to change their minds when necessary. Daniel's influence was such that he left people different from when he first found them. Two of the three kings we know had their values dramatically altered by Daniel; the third, Belshazzar, at least heard the unvarnished truth about what he'd done to precipitate the collapse of his throne.

When we think of leadership, we naturally assume formal situations where someone is in charge, setting direction, picking good people, making things happen. But leadership begins with the desire to influence.

All Christ-followers have the opportunity, sooner or later, to be influential in the real world of the streets. Herein lies one of the unique challenges: the recognition that the man or woman of God is not to be a passive person. Each of us has been called as we follow Christ into the weekdays to exert kingdom influence on others.

In the early 1800s England underwent a revolution. It was not violent like the one that happened during the same era in France. The revolution ushered in the great Victorian period during which there was an explosion of institutions committed to the education and assistance of the poor. Behind the revolution was a spiritual renewal in which many men and women came to understand what it meant to follow Christ.

One little-known but significant factor in this revolution was the role of England's nannies, the women (usually from the poorer families) who were hired by the upper classes to care for children. Many of these nannies were Christ-followers, and they taught the children about Jesus. They also influenced the wives of England's leaders regarding the love of Christ and the plight of England's poor. These women in turn began to expose their husbands to what they were learning. The result? Laws were passed in Parliament, and organizations were founded that made a great difference in the way of English life. And not a little of it can be attributed to the nannies who decided to become leaders where it counted.

In New York City we meet modern-day nannies all the time who are caring for the children of bivocational families. They come from all over the United States and Europe. And some of them are Christ-followers. Everything the nineteenth-century nannies of Victorian England achieved through their influence in the nursery is achievable today.

Christ-followers are like that when they follow the Lord into the weekdays.

8. Loyalty

Daniel was faithful.

The book of Daniel doesn't give us any pictures of Daniel as a leisure-oriented man. One can't imagine him, for example, heading out to a soccer game with the king or playing racquetball with some of his associates. Daniel seems out of place at a party or at the theater. We can only imagine that somewhere along the line he found time to intersect on a more informal basis with some people in his world. Apart from the original three Jerusalem colleagues who entered the king's school with him, we have no idea who his friends were.

But we can assume these things about his working relationships. On a day-to-day basis, he knew who signed his paycheck and who deserved his loyalty: the kings he served.

It's never quite said, but one has the strong feeling throughout the account of Daniel's life that he felt called by God to help these men become successful. More than once the contemporary business literature has suggested that a primary goal of every person ought to be to make his or her boss become successful. This principle has to be applied carefully, of course, but Daniel apparently believed in it. He saw these kings as men who ruled under Heaven's purposes, therefore, to assist them was to be in accord with those purposes.

Faithfulness meant being ready to provide what the king asked for: leading a major division of the king's administration, interpreting a dream, offering wise counsel about handwriting on a wall, dependably auditing a governmental system.

Faithfulness also meant absolute candor when the truth had to be told. One broods on the courage of Daniel when he had to go before Nebuchadnezzar and tell him bad news.

A small hint of Daniel's respect and perhaps affection is revealed in these words:

> Daniel . . . was greatly perplexed for a time, and his thoughts terrified him. So the king said, "[Daniel] do not let the dream or its meaning alarm you."
> [Daniel] answered, "My lord, if only the dream applied to your enemies and its meaning to your adversaries!" (Dan. 4:19).

Even though he felt badly about what he discerned in the king's dream, Daniel did not shrink from being the spokesman for what had to be said. This is the ultimate test of loyalty. Interpreting the dream to its fullest extent, Daniel told the king what he needed to hear: "Therefore, O king, be pleased to accept my advice: Renounce your sins by doing what is right, and your wickedness by being kind to the oppressed. It may be that then your prosperity will continue" (Dan. 4:27).

Nebuchadnezzar didn't follow Daniel's advice at first. But after he had suffered the promised consequences for a while, he got the point.

Two kings later, Daniel found himself in that lions' den because others wanted him out of the way. When he emerged the following morning and reported to the anxious king, his words were those of a faithful man: "O king, live forever! My God sent his angel, and he shut the mouths of the lions. They have not hurt me, because I was found innocent in his sight. Nor have I ever done any wrong before you, O king" (Dan. 6:21–22).

Centuries later, St. Paul would write to Christ-followers about life during the weekdays: "Whatever you do, work at it with all your heart, as working for the Lord, not for men, since you know that you will receive an inheritance from the Lord as a reward. It is the Lord Christ you are serving" (Col. 3:23–24).

Daniel fulfilled those words as nearly perfectly as anyone ever could. His work was characterized by real-world faith, and every task, as a result, had sacred implications.

The story of Daniel in the courts of four pagan kings is a thrilling one. In the beginning we're told, "And Daniel remained [lasted] there until the first year of King Cyrus." Toward the end of the story we're told, "So Daniel prospered during the reign of Darius and the reign of Cyrus the Persian."

When someone reaches his hundredth birthday, it is customary to ask the secret of his longevity. The answers are often amusing. But ask Daniel the secret of his longevity in a harsh and godless environment where he not only survived but thrived, and I think he'll walk you through a few of these weekday kingdom qualities.

When Christ leads us into the real world and challenges us to forge a faith that can operate with value on the streets during the weekdays, Daniel's way of doing things may be exactly what He has in mind.

CHAPTER TWENTY

Macrochallenge

A Thought for You, Smithy
The place where you are forging your faith is a tiny part of a big world, Smithy. But you're in charge of that portion of the world, and you can make it a place where people love to come and find light.

In his book *Odyssey*, John Sculley writes of his career decision to move from being president of Pepsi-Cola to being president and CEO of Apple Computer. There was nothing simple about the choice, Sculley says.

Pepsi was a well-established, prestigious company, and John Sculley was only one person away from the top of the entire conglomerate. Apple, on the other hand, was locked in a struggle to survive; at best it had an "iffy" future in the volatile, highly competitive world of computer manufacturing. Sculley had years of successful experience in marketing beverages; he didn't have the slightest idea how one revived sagging computer sales. So why exchange a sure thing for a high risk?

There wouldn't have even been a decision to make if it had not been for one man. Several times Steve Jobs, the brilliant but impulsive founder of Apple, had flown from California's Silicon Valley to New York City to persuade Sculley to join him.

Jobs was in New York again, Sculley writes, and the two met, first for lunch and then a continuing conversation outdoors on the balcony of a high-rise apartment building. As usual, the subject matter focused on the merits of Apple's offer, and Jobs became increasingly persistent.

As the two gazed out on the cityscape (I am reminded of Jesus and

193

Satan looking upon the nations from a mountaintop), the choice-making question once again came Sculley's way. "Are you going to come to Apple?" Steve Jobs asked.

"Steve," Sculley says he replied, "I really love what you're doing [at Apple]. I'm excited by it, how could anyone not be captivated? But it just doesn't make sense."

Sculley went on attempting to discourage Jobs by suggesting that Apple probably wasn't prepared to pay the kind of salary he would need to match the relative security he presently enjoyed at Pepsi. When asked what that salary might be, Sculley casually mentioned a million dollars annually, a million more for a signing bonus, and the promise of a further million in severance pay if things at Apple did not work out.

At first Jobs was incredulous, and he asked how Sculley had come up with such figures.

"They're nice big round numbers . . ." was part of the answer.

But Jobs wasn't prepared to let that stop the conversation and said so. Apple would be willing to pay the kind of money Sculley was describing, he said, even if it had to come from his (Jobs's) own pocket. The decision was once again Sculley's to make, and again he demurred.

Steve Jobs was exasperated, and in his frustration he asked one more question, the one that finally caused John Sculley to make one of the most talked-about corporate moves in modern American business.

He asked, "Do you want to spend the rest of your life selling sugared water or do you want a chance to change the world?"

"It was as if someone reached up and delivered a stiff blow to my stomach," writes John Sculley. The question simply eroded all his resistance, and it made him think like a dreamer or a visionary. After all, changing the world is a heady thought.

The reasons for saying no to Steve Jobs had to do with a preoccupation with the potential loss of pensions and deferred compensation, whether or not life in California was compatible with his personal tastes, and other items that—as he admitted—preoccupy the value systems of middle-aged people. Hardly change-the-world issues.

Sculley comments, "The question was a monstrous one: one for which I had no answer. It simply knocked the wind out of me."

Sculley is clearly a romantic. It would take a change-the-world challenge like that to capture his imagination. I'm probably just like him. He and I are vulnerable to "monstrous questions" like the one posed on the apartment balcony. Other people, less inclined toward romantic notions and more amenable to objective facts, wouldn't be.

Nevertheless, when you think about it, there is some kind of question or theme that, if presented at the right time and in the right way, will press most of us to take a careful look at the direction in which we are traveling in life and to consider the possibility of change. I call these *the macroquestions* or *the macrothemes:* proposals to do something daring and unusual that may, as a result, reorient our direction in life, reshuffle our values, and affect our attitude toward much of our routines.

The story of almost every outstanding biblical personality begins with a version of the macros. As men and women forged their real-world faith, they acquired some sense of the grandeur of God and worshiped. As a result, they began to acknowledge an awareness of inner emptiness or lostness and repented.

This twofold experience laid the groundwork for insight into how they could become something or do something useful for their generation. Though they had no pretensions concerning the gloominess of their worlds—the difficulty, sadness, complexity, danger, and unfairness of life—they saw the opportunity to bring light to that darkness, to make a difference. And they set out to make a little history in the name of their God!

Their motivations were never to become notorious or wealthy or powerful. Rather, they were pulled by a dream, if you please; a dream implanted in the heart by God's Spirit; a dream of what a piece of reclaimed creation might look like if it was touched by the authority and power of Christ. No matter how small their sphere of influence, this they could do.

A crucial part of real-world faith building, then, is a personal decision to connect one's life to an overarching dream or a consuming idea. But it must be a dream or an idea splendid and powerful enough to become germane to every particle of daily life—not only extraordinary events that happen occasionally, but a dream including the endless stream of experiences we often refer to as routine and humdrum. Even they must be seen as utterly Christian in the context of real-world faith. All too often, they are not!

Here I am forced to face the limited nature of my own history-making faith. Too often I am tempted to separate out the things I do into faith and nonfaith categories or to refer to them as sacred and secular. Such a division should never exist in my mind if everything has sacred implications.

For centuries, people have speculated about the key change that Jesus instigated in the lives of His followers when He came to this world. I believe the key change was the dream He gave them—the dream of the kingdom of God.

The concept of the kingdom was nothing new to His disciples, of course. Each of them had been brought up to fantasize about it. So the idea was not new; but Jesus' teaching was.

They conceived the kingdom to be a restoration of the old political entity that David and other kings had once ruled. They dreamed of an overthrow of the Roman oppressor, of more comfortable times, of a renewed position of respect in the family of nearby kingdoms. Perhaps they even thought of the kingdom as a place where they might enjoy a bit of privilege and recognition. Who knows what really went on in their minds the first time they heard Jesus discuss the kingdom?

It is clear that they carried their preconceptions through almost all of the three years they walked with the Lord. And when He said "kingdom," they simply overlaid His words with their prejudices.

Then one day He told them a story that must have shaken them to the roots, for the story suggested an entirely different concept of the kingdom. They were thinking politics; Jesus was thinking task. They were thinking privilege; Jesus was thinking servanthood. They were thinking power; Jesus was thinking accountability. They were thinking ownership; Jesus was thinking stewardship. The story Jesus told slashed across all their preconceptions.

A prince, He said, left on an extended trip. His task was to obtain certification from higher authorities, authorizing him to rule over a kingdom.

During his absence, the prince arranged for his assets to be placed in the hands of trusted, able servants for the purposes of protection and investment. What he did was routine in those times. There were no banks, so wealthy people often made such a distribution and hoped for the best.

In the prince's case, Jesus said, the servants were not to merely protect what had been consigned to them; they were to invest it with an eye toward making profit. "Trade with this until I return" was the mission. High earnings were anticipated.

I can almost hear Jesus illustrating the prince's instructions to his servants. Take my money and buy old farms and bring them back to operating order. Acquire promising but struggling businesses and re-store them to profitable conditions. Purchase undeveloped property and add value to it. *Wherever you do this, you introduce my authority and control; you establish my effective presence in those places.*

The acquisitions were meant to become enclaves where the authority of the absent prince was acknowledged as lord. You could say that the servants of the prince were to press his authority into sites and locations throughout the land. And so wherever they did this, the kingdom of the prince existed right there at that very moment.

The prince returned much later, Jesus' story continued, and when he did, he called for an auditing of the assets and the profits. Several servants reported remarkable earnings; one did not.

The prince was delighted with and generous toward those who were profitable; he was outraged with and punitive toward the servant who did nothing but sit on his hands. Protection of assets had not been the prince's challenge; profit had been.

There is much more to the story, but this is enough. What is important is the point toward which Jesus was leading His disciples. It described the history-making mission of the Christ-follower in a real world.

The story foresaw Jesus' departure from the earth, like the prince, for an indefinite period of time. It also anticipated an unannounced date when He would return. And when He did, He would carry with Him the authority to assert lordship over all the earth, a mandate given to Him by the Heavenly Father.

But what of the interim period? What was the role of the prince and his servants between the departure and the return?

The secret was in the investment of the assets. Wherever they were invested, there the prince's authority would be established. The point Jesus was trying to make with the disciples was this: I am going to leave you soon, and when I do, each of you will have assets, and your mission is to invest them. Wherever you invest the assets, there my authority and lordship will be established.

The assets? Things He had taught them through word and deed; empowerment through the gift of the Holy Spirit; a new view of the world and the purposes driving it; a model of fearlessness concerning human structures and systems; the opportunity to set the stage for future generations to discover more and more about God's purposes for creation.

In my judgment, no story or teaching in the New Testament makes the role of the Christ-follower in the real world clearer than this one. Each of us is a servant. Each of us has been entrusted with assets belonging to the Prince. The assets include our skills, capacities, energies, what some call spiritual gifts, relationships, and opportunities. Every day as we enter into the real world, our task is a simple one: we press the authority of the Prince of Heaven into the dark places of the world.

In his wonderful book *Life Together,* Dietrich Bonhoeffer quotes Martin Luther:

> The Kingdom is to be in the midst of your enemies. And he who will not suffer this does not want to be of the Kingdom of Christ; *he wants to be among friends, to sit among roses and lilies, not with the bad people but the devout people.* O you blasphemers and betrayers of Christ! If Christ had done what you are doing who would have ever been spared? (Emphasis mine)

As I cross over to Second Avenue on the tram each morning, I have a way of looking at the real world in front of me with all of its sights and sounds and people that brings everything into focus. I am to press the authority of the One I follow, Christ, into every transaction. Luther is correct. To sit among the lilies and the devout people may be safe, but it is not kingdom activity. Incidentally, where would I be if Christ had not come to the "Second Avenue" where I live?

An encounter with the man who serves me coffee (decaffeinated) and a grapefruit at the Tramway Cafe is a chance to press Christ's authority into the conversation by my attitude, my appreciation, or even my affirmation of the way he does his job.

The choice to greet an obviously lonely elderly person on the street is a chance to press Christ's authority into the void in her life.

The way I conduct my business over the phone when I am shabbily treated, the dignity with which I treat a subordinate, the caring I show for a customer, the quality of the work I give to my employer, and the excellence with which I achieve my tasks over and above expectations are all ways in which Christ's authority is pressed into a world normally dominated by disorder and rebellion.

It is possible in many of the cases I have just mentioned that soon after I leave there will be a return to disorder. The next person in the life of the waiter at the cafe may be abusive. The aging person may once more feel loneliness ten minutes later. I cannot be discouraged by this. My task is to do the Master's bidding and assume that all things come under His sovereign control.

In this way, every action in my life becomes meaningful. I don't have to speak a religious vocabulary or do religious things to follow Christ. All of life becomes Christ-following when I am conscious that I am a servant of the Prince and I am establishing His authority wherever I go.

Many of us who have been believers for a long time were not brought up to see the making of kingdom history in this way. The instruction we received boiled down to this: the only serious issue is to do the work of an evangelist. The world was not our home, the old gospel song said; we were just passing through.

We didn't fully understand that making kingdom history might mean carrying Christ's presence into the political arena, into the educational system, into the marketplace, and into the arts. Admittedly, the cutting edge of the word of Christ is to proclaim His saving work on the cross so that people might believe and become Christ-followers also. But many of us didn't understand that that was only the beginning. And that all other activities weren't secular. They too were sacred if we entered them as servants of the Prince using our assets to establish His presence.

Some did not see clearly enough that real-world faith is not an avenue to full-time Christian service. It is, rather, an agenda in which every bit of one's life becomes meaningful in terms of pressing Christ's presence and authority into otherwise dark situations.

Gail and I take a late afternoon walk. Here and there she stops to pick up a beer can or a piece of paper. "I'm pressing Christ's presence into disorder," she remarks (parroting my manuscript). And I join her in this effort, even though I frequently kid her and begin to call her St. Gail of the Trashcan.

But Gail has taught me that even the effort one makes at beautification is an act of reconciling the environment to the order that God intended for creation to have. She has demonstrated that even the simple routine of cleaning something—a house, a lawn, or a street—has sacred implications when we understand that restoring things to order is a kingdom activity.

Bruce Larson must have been thinking similarly when he wrote about his friend, Gert Behanna, "one of God's most remarkable characters." When Larson wrote these words, she was still alive and involved in a vigorous life of speaking and counseling:

This woman had run through five husbands, was an alcoholic, attempted suicide, and got converted in her fifties. She now travels around the country speaking to groups almost every day of the year. She is responsible for thousands of people coming to know the Lord who so changed her. When we met recently, I said, "Gert, what have you been doing lately?"

"Well," she said, "I travel around a lot, Bruce, as you know, and I used to get so disgusted about the dirty restrooms in gas stations. To go into most of them, you've got to wear galoshes. Each time I used one, I complained to the Lord about how this servant of his was being treated.

"Then one day Jesus seemed to be saying to me, 'Gert, in as much as you've done it unto me . . .' I said, 'Lord, you mean you use these restrooms too?' When I realized that he would be the next person who'd be coming into the gas station restroom after me, I knew I'd better do something about it. Now when I go into a messy restroom, I pick up all the towels and stuff them into the wastebasket. I take the towel and wipe off the mirror and the sink and the toilet seat. I leave the place looking as clean as possible and I say, 'Well, Lord, there it is; I hope you enjoy it.'"

Accepting my role as a servant to properly handle the assets of the Prince brings a real-world meaning to my faith. It causes me to think ecologically about my responsibility for Christ's environment. It prompts me to think economically when I weigh the responsibility I have in spending and using my money. It causes me to think intellectually as I attempt to put my mind to work at the highest possible level. It moves me to think politically as I ask myself what can I do to contribute to a system that, if kept honest and focused, will benefit people whom God loves very much.

It is enjoyable to consider what a greater world under the reign of the Prince would be like, where all things—humanity, living things, the stuff of creation—might exist as they were meant to be in the creative mind of God. Such a dream is not idle fantasy. It answers to something I believe is hidden within each of us: a memory deep in our spiritual genes that knew of a time when God came down and walked with man, and everything was good. And the dream also answers a hope deep within us—some have called it a healthy homesickness—that one day all things will be restored to their original creative intent by the hand of God.

Believing that this is exactly what will happen when the Prince returns in glorious triumph, the servant of the kingdom makes a little history each day by claiming hunks of a spoiled creation and establishing Christ's presence in it. It cannot be done permanently (picked-up streets get dirty again, and reformed political systems do get corrupt again, and work done well the first time has to be done over and over again), but it can be done with the conviction that it makes a statement and brings Christ to places where He might otherwise never have been known.

A recent series of articles in the *New York Times* has described the unprecedented shift of Latin American people from the Catholic church to the Protestant charismatic community. In many Central American countries, estimates range as high as 30 percent of the population now settled in evangelical charismatic communions. But critics of the movement say this shift is not good news. They suggest that the faith style of evangelicals encourages a withdrawal from the affairs of the real world (my words). They express alarm that this makes it easier for dictatorial governments to press their will upon the people and keep power.

If this was at all true (and the evidence is not convincing), it would be alarming. First, because it does not parallel what we know about biblical personalities who confronted crooked kings and leaders and agitated for change in the most forceful ways. Second, because it does not square with Christian performance in other postbiblical centuries when men and women who followed the Lord were at the spear point of great changes. But, I must observe, the criticism does reflect a tendency of Western evangelicals to be less than active in the political, educational, and cultural systems and structures of our communities.

The dream of the kingdom is no small agenda! Taken seriously, it pervades every dimension of a Christ-follower's life. How one treats family or roommates in the early morning hours; how one behaves in the morning commute; how one intersects with associates in the workplace; how one treats the stranger; how one makes choices to expend personal resources; what part one chooses to play in community life; and what positions one takes in the formation of public policy. And these are only a few of the obvious ones.

The person in the process of forging a real-world faith dreams of change and restoration not only because he ponders what could be but also because he knows that the spirit pervading much of our time is destructive. Like Jesus weeping over the arrogant city of Jerusalem, the person who dreams the dream of the kingdom grieves over the unraveling of our beautiful world. He is not a cynic, and he is not a chronic complainer (an all-too-easy thing for any of us to become when we are eager for change). He loves the world because he learns that God loves the world, and if he is a critic about its present downward spiral, he is a repentant critic who acknowledges joint responsibility. His perspective on things going sour is similar to the prayer of Nehemiah who, when he heard of the deplorable state of a ruined Jerusalem, prayed, "I and my fathers have sinned."

In the midst of all of this history, the camera focuses for a moment on you and me. We follow Christ; we listen to His Father; we seek the grace of the Spirit's empowerment. Where in all of this can we make some history, make a difference, leave things a bit better than they were when we got here?

If we can do kingdom work only after we leave work and head for other places, there are very few hours of the week in which anything at all can be done. But if we can appreciate how every moment of the day has kingdom implications in the perspective of the Creator, something new has happened. A macroquestion takes over and aligns everything we do with a higher purpose.

A senior vice president of a New York bank told me about his harrowing experience on a commuter train. A man, obviously drunk, sat across the aisle and began to harass him. "At first I simply ignored him," my friend said. "But then he became obsessed with getting my attention, and it looked as if it was going to be a contest of our wills."

"Hey," the drunk shouted, "you think I'm drunk, don't you?"

"'Yeah,' I said, 'you are,' and I went back to my paper, hoping the matter would drop. But it didn't."

"Get out of here; I want you out of that seat and out of this car now," the intoxicated man said, and there being no conductor available, the situation became tense.

I put down my paper, my friend said, and looked at this man straight in the eye. I said, "You know, God really loves you," and somehow the words and the way I said them broke his nasty spirit.

He came across the aisle and sat next to me. "My mother used to talk like that," he said. And the two began to talk quietly. When they reached the station in Manhattan, they talked for a while longer. The drunk slowly came off his high and listened to an executive who took the time to tell him that he was important to God and that there were ways and places to get help.

"We exchanged phone numbers, and I talked to him every few days for several months. We're out of touch now, and I don't know what's happened to him. But I never forgot that chance to break through the hostility and bring the man to some sense of peace."

The kingdom was being built in that conversation.

The president of a company hears of a young single mother with two children whose husband is unwilling to maintain his obligations of child support. He finds her a job in the telemarketing department, ensures that she has flex-time hours so that she can be with her children during most of their off-school hours. I watch her gain an increasing sense of confidence that she can meet her obligations and not have to cave in to seeking welfare or making choices that might bring short-term relief but long-term disaster. The company president has been kingdom building.

In the heart of New York City is a dry cleaning establishment my wife, Gail, frequents on almost a weekly basis. I've heard her talk about it several times.

"The first time I went in I knew that there was something different about the place," Gail usually tells friends. "In the city you get used to being treated as if you're nothing in a lot of businesses. But then you come into this store, and you're greeted as if they'd been waiting for you all day long. I almost think I want to get something dirty so that I can have a reason to stop in there. They always have a cheerful word, despite the fact that the cleaning machinery makes the store unbearably hot and humid.

"By the third time I'd stopped in, the men who run the cleaners knew my name. They always have my cleaning ready, and the quality of the work is excellent."

What's going on at that establishment? Is it just good business or a greater dream?

"One day when I was there," Gail says, "I said to Larry, who works the counter, 'You really make it a treat to come here. What's the secret behind your upbeat mood?'

"He surprised me when he said, 'I'm a Christian, and I figure that that's how Christians are supposed to treat customers.'"

As I said, I've listened to Gail tell this story about the men at the cleaners several times. And it has occurred to both of us that this is a place where hundreds of people come each week and return again and again. And one man in particular has decided that this is at least one place in New York where they will have a unique experience. Not every one of them will know it, but they are in a place stamped with the presence of Christ. In other words, when you take your clothes there, you don't just go to the cleaners; you walk into a little piece of the kingdom, and a servant who works there is making that possible.

John Sculley writes in his book about how he left all the security of a gigantic corporation to go to California. Why? To change the world, of course. Nothing else would have gotten him to go. And others, like Peter, leave a paid-for fishing boat in lovely backwater Galilee or, like Saul of Tarsus, walk away from a cushy position in the religious establishment of Jerusalem. Why? To change their worlds, of course. People do interesting things when a dream is involved. Some dreams, like global computerization, are noble. But other dreams, like making kingdom history, are eternal.

CHAPTER TWENTY-ONE

What's in the Box?

A Thought for You, Smithy
Smithy, even the way you do your work reflects
your growing faith. Get into the habit of asking
yourself, What does my work mean? What values
does it reflect? What does the quality of my labor
say about me and the One who called me to this
assignment?

Among my special friends is a man my age who has enjoyed unusual prosperity in his business. He is a Christ-follower and has set himself to learning as much as he can about what Christ expects of him in the use of his skills and his profits.

A few years ago my friend made a decision to curb the growth of his business so that he could devote more time to other missions in life that had to do with the development of people. His decision was not designed to remove him from the marketplace, for it was there that he felt he could have his most significant kingdom influence. Rather, it was part of a personal strategy that ensured balance for him personally and a chance to be involved in other things beyond the office. Because he has done this, many men and women around the world have profited intellectually and spiritually from his generosity.

Since we live in different parts of the country, much of our contact is by telephone. I am always stimulated by our long talks, which (fortunately for me and my phone bill) are usually initiated by him.

In one such conversation he described a business opportunity he had been considering. Some investors were collaborating to acquire a major property that was sure to provide a handsome return, and he was being invited into the deal as a "major player." His jumping in would have required a substantial investment of money and an equally heavy investment of time that was already budgeted for his mission of people development.

"This has been a tough decision," he told me. "The challenge alone of making that deal work is stimulating enough," he said. "But the potential payoff on the investment is enough to make your head spin."

"So what's stopping you?" I asked over the phone.

"I have a couple of factors influencing my decision. My life-plan isn't compatible with this thing. And the Lord: He's been speaking to me. Know how He's done it?"

I said I was curious, so he continued.

"I'm on a plane flying to Washington last week. Guess who's sitting across the aisle from me?" He went on to mention the name of an official who heads a major United States government agency, one that has a lot to do with the very business he was thinking about.

"So I tell him about the deal that's cooking and ask him what he thinks. Oh, and I also tell him about my life-plan and ask if he can see any way in which the deal and the plan are harmonious. Do you know what he said to me?"

I didn't know.

"This is what he said, I swear, word for word: 'It seems to me that you are standing on a mountaintop, and this is your temptation.' The minute he said that I knew I was being asked to bow down to someone. The only question was to whom? Jesus or the other guy? It didn't take long before I knew who it was in this case, and so the minute we landed in D.C., I went to the Madison Hotel, made a call, and was out of the whole thing. So it was back to the mission."

My friend has said yes to a lot of deals. And most of them have been enormously successful. The result has been the kind of financial benefits you would expect. I've met more than a few people who work in his world, and I've seen most of them become addicted to "doing deals" like the one he described. Money ceases to be the primary driving influence because they just ache to win *one more time*. In fact, the money involved becomes little more than a way of keeping a score of the winnings.

This story inspires me because my friend shows the evidences of real-world faith. His life-plan has acknowledged the priority of knowing God. His decision suggests self-mastery, the ability to say a strategic no when others would have said yes. His choices are those of a kingdom servant who has a dream to press Christ's power and presence into the lives of people.

What I appreciate most about my friend is his serious effort to place Christ right in the midst of his vocational activity. He'd be the first to acknowledge occasional errors of judgment, I'm sure, but there is no doubt in my mind that he has decided that where he works, what he does, and how he does it will be the front line of kingdom effort for him.

On another occasion when we visited, he told me of a recent conference he had had with a man who is an internationally known consultant in strategic long-range planning for businesses and government. The purpose of the consultation had to do with the planning of my friend's business activities.

"We examined all aspects of my company, and then we took at look at my life-plan," he said, describing the flow of the meeting. "And then he took a piece of paper and drew a box in the middle of it. He said to me, 'I've been listening to you for about two hours now. And it all comes down to one of two things. Christ or money: You tell me what's in that box—the Christ of your life-plan or money. Because your entire long-range plan works outward from that box. When you tell me what's in there, Christ or money, I'll tell you exactly how to plan your future.'"

I think this man has a little "Daniel" in him. He is conscious that he works for a higher authority, the God of Jesus Christ. He has this strong conviction that his material and spiritual assets are not his but the Lord's and that they better be properly managed. He has a life-plan carefully thought out and evaluated by people he trusts. And he has a hunger to grow and finish very, very strong. I believe he is in the process of forging a real-world faith.

Because I now live and do most of my work right in the marketplace, I am forced to spend a lot of time thinking about what difference Jesus makes when He is Lord of our careers. When I lived in the suburbs, I spent a lot of time talking about Christ in community life: getting along with neighbors and how much time one should spend with his or her children, and how busy we should or shouldn't be at church. But now my parish is located where people work, and their questions have forced me, as never before, to wrestle with these issues.

As I've mentioned before, I most often eat my weekday breakfasts at the Tramway Cafe or the Silver Star, both on Second Avenue in the heart of Manhattan. There I sit with people who are headed to an office down on Wall Street or at midtown. And what do we talk about?How a job that seemed so exciting at age thirty-two is so boring at thirty-nine. Why greed is such a driving factor in so many businesses. What one does if he or she works for a nasty boss. How does one live with negative stress? How wrong should something be before you put your job on the line and blow the whistle? What do you do if you know beyond a doubt that there is sexism or racism driving certain hiring decisions? How do you balance the priorities of personal life, home, and work when you are competing against others who are willing to sacrifice all of it for another dollar?

The questions at the Tramway Cafe do not stop there. How loudly do you scream if your company reneges on a bonus it promised six months ago? How do you handle a working relationship with a member of the opposite sex when you're attracted to the person but shouldn't be? How can a Christ-follower work in a business when you know that your success is going to mean another person's failure? Is there any way to lift the values of a company so that it sees its purposes as more than simply profit? How do we elevate the environment of the workplace so that people grow and enjoy what they do?

One other question seems to arise more frequently than the others. Someone asks, What would you say if I told you that I'm thinking of leaving my job and going into the ministry?

I love the pastoral ministry, and I have mentored more than a few young men and women who have heard the call of God and moved in that direction. But when the question comes, I am more frequently given to talking people out of such a move unless there has been such an unmistakable mandate that it can be neither denied nor resisted. I do this because I am convinced that the kingdom of God is powerfully represented by people who "last" like Daniel in the marketplace and choose to live as he did.

I came to see that behind this question is a common confusion about whether or not Christ walks through the marketplace with people and makes a difference through them. And if He does, how does He do it? Some Christ-followers have a difficult time seeing the value of their work in kingdom terms. They feel as if they must be wasting precious time serving a business when they could be working in a totally Christian vocation.

And that has led me to formulate some questions to stimulate thought for how one can bring the kingdom of Christ to a place of work. Since they have become a familiar agenda at breakfast in the Tramway Cafe, I have called them:

The Tramway Questions

1. Are you maximizing your past experiences?

What past experiences and natural gifts has God providentially deposited in your life (education, learning experiences, expertise, successes and failures), and how can these be strategically used to improve the quality of life in the place where you work? Have you tried to see how everything in your life up to now could be strategic preparation for the kingdom contributions you could make today and in days to come?

2. Are you an asset or a liability?

In your working world, what does it mean to be more of a giver than a taker when it comes to adding value to your employer's interest? Does your employer consider you a distinct asset to the business so that, aside from your "niceness" as a person, you are worth (perhaps even more than) what he pays you?

3. Are you managing the routines?

What does it mean to stamp Christ's presence in your present vocational situation? In other words, if Christ were to sit at your desk, make your rounds, sell your widgets, type your letters, or provide your service, what would be the general tenor of the atmosphere? Is your organization a better place to work because you are on the payroll?

4. Do you know which issues you are prepared to stand for, no matter what?

What key decisions will you be called to make or influence, either independently or in concert with others, that will make a significant difference in the direction your organization will take in the future? Can you identify the signal issues that would cause you to bet your career and your personal security?

5. Are you in a position to spread Christ-following values?

What values will you identify with and "evangelize" among your colleagues and associates? Have you ever taken time to list what they are? Do you read or study to see what other Christ-following men and women consider to be values for the marketplace? Are you alert to those times in your workplace when significant values are being violated? Will you be a passive operator, reacting to things when they come at you, or will you become wise and proactive, pressing for values higher than the "bottom line"?

6. What is the nature of your influence on key relationships?

What are your realistic hopes and goals in affecting people in key relationships with you? Think of your superiors, peers, subordinates, customers, professional colleagues, the stockholders. Will any dimension of their lives be enlarged (even to experience the love of Christ) because they have intersected with you? Who are you mentoring? Who are you influencing? Who are you encouraging? Who are you restraining from making poor choices? Are people nudged a bit closer to God because they've had the chance to come alongside you?

7. How do you handle your power and your success?

How do you practice the showing of respect toward, and how do you provide opportunities for, the development and advancement of those who are in positions of relative powerlessness? And if you are regarded as successful in your world, how are you managing the prestige, the power, and the influence? If you are a "big guy," how do you ensure that you never lose touch with the "little guy"? And if everyone is beginning to look up to you, do you respect the "leverage" you have in others' lives and use it to bring attention to greater things than yourself?

8. Are you maintaining life's balances?

What will you do to ensure that your working patterns and priorities are held in a reasonable balance with other sectors—key relationships in family, personal growth and development, Sabbath, the Christ-following community? Do you have a life-plan (beyond your business plan) whose bottom line is similar to the one written about Jesus? ("And Jesus grew in wisdom and stature, and in favor with God and men" [Luke 2:52].)

9. What do your spiritual disciplines look like?

How do you regularly engage in monitoring and developing your inner space? Are you capable of hearing its signals when God triggers messages of warning, rebuke, affirmation, or guidance? Are you forcing the schedule open so that there is adequate time for the ordering of your private world so that God is free to visit there?

10. To whom have you made yourself accountable for personal and spiritual growth?

Are there two or three friends (of the same gender) whose judgment you trust, with whom you deal in total openness and frankness, to whom you listen, and whose approval is important to you? Who are the whistle-blowers to get your attention if they tell you that you are out of balance, misusing your position or possessions, or that they fear for your relationship with God?

11. Do you practice disciplined stewardship?

What are you doing with the fruits of your labor: your income, your resulting possessions, your leisure? Are you on an unending spiral of materialistic expansion, or can you practice the disciplines of "downward mobility" and upward generosity? Are you paying strict attention to the fact that your money, your influence, and your skill belong to God and that the books on your use of everything are being carefully kept until the day of evaluation before the throne of God?

12. Has your real-world faith helped some people to become Christ-followers?

Who is being spiritually influenced because he or she works with you every day? Have you developed genuine enough relationships with your colleagues so that a conversation about Christ might be a natural topic? Is there anything about the uniqueness of your Christ-following life that would make another person curious about what drives you?

13. Quo Vadis: where are you going?

Do you have a life-plan that spells out your commitments, your mission, your standards of performance, and your awareness of your limitations and weaknesses? Do you know where you believe God wants you to go with your life so that your goals are bigger than your job? If you don't develop a plan, someone else will do it for you. So when do you get started?

A few years ago a man asked if he could visit me at my home. We were not well acquainted, but we had many common acquaintances. It was clear that he was on the verge of losing his emotional stability. The pressures of a struggling marriage, a feeling of failure in life (despite his business success), and declining health were eating away at his will to live. We talked for hours, and I struggled to give him what he needed. Frankly, a lot of my stock answers didn't seem to penetrate his inner wall of despair.

This man had become addicted to profit. Three times he had built successful businesses and then walked away from them because of the increased stress in his life. Each time he began again he had vowed to slow down and balance his business life with other priorities. But he apparently could not walk away from one more deal when it stared him in the face and asked him to bow.

On another day we met for a meal. As we drove toward the place to eat, we came to a point on the interstate where we could see the buildings he had built, which housed his most recent flourishing business. Everything on that property was a monument to achievements that people, who think success is everything, would want.

As we drove past the property, I said to him, "You must be very proud of all this." And I meant what I said because I admired the substantial nature of his effort. I shall never forget his response.

"I hate every square foot of it. It's cost me my marriage, my family, my health, and my relationship with God. I wish I'd never seen any part of it."

In less than a year he was dead, more of a broken heart than anything else. Given a normal lifetime, he should have had thirty more years.

Could there have been a time in his life when thinking through something like the Tramway Questions might have helped? I don't know. I like to think they would have.

More than 150 years ago, an English clergyman, John Caird, preached a sermon in the presence of Queen Victoria. She was so moved by what he said that she requested that his remarks be expanded and printed. In the sermon Caird addressed the matter of real-world faith in the nineteenth-century marketplace.

Caird told his audience, "A Christlike spirit will Christianize everything it touches. To spiritualize what is material, to Christianize what is secular—this is a noble achievement." It is indeed a noble achievement to follow Christ into the workplace and pursue the goal of establishing the kingdom at every step. "To Christianize," using Caird's language, means to initiate Christ's presence and authority in each transaction.

Two men, friends of mine, make two different sets of decisions. The one who is gone now had all the talent and skill of the one who is still alive and growing. What's the difference between the two? I think it has everything to do with what is in the box: Christ or profit?

CHAPTER TWENTY-TWO

Putting Something Back on the Truck

A Thought for You, Smithy
Don't quit, Smithy. Never! Never! Never! The
Giver of faith will one day acknowledge your ef-
forts with indescribable rewards, and you will
know that everything was worth it all. Yours is a
faith made for the real world.

On the weekend, not long ago, I was working through a final draft of this book in my office on Sixty-first Street. I was the only one in the building at the time, and so I picked up the phone when it rang. The man at the other end sounded upset.

"This is Dr. A——, the podiatrist. I have an office in the building next door to you."

I'd never met or seen the doctor, but I walked past his office almost every day and had seen his name in the window enough times to recognize it when he told me who he was. So I asked what I could do for him.

"My son has a problem. He needs to get a prescription from the pharmacy quickly; he doesn't have enough money, and I'm about an hour's drive away from there. Is there anyone who could loan him the money until I can get there?"

"Sure," I said without hesitation. "I'll take care of your son. Just tell him to push the buzzer at the office door; I'll be waiting for him."

The doctor could not have been more thankful. "Reverend, I want you to know how much I appreciate your trust and your willingness to help us in a tough spot. You must be quite some guy."

I returned to my writing with a good feeling in my heart about that

214

call. This was kingdom servanthood: real-world faith in action. I was going to be able to help a neighbor who needed a hand, and I would doubtless make a new friend on the block, someone who would probably tell others about the kindness of the man at the church.

When the doctor called, I was working on the part of the book proposing that life is, among other things, difficult, unfair, complex, and not a little sad. How many times I had been tempted to delete that section, worrying that some readers would reject my perspective, thinking it to be too depressing.

But each time I overcame the temptation, choosing to leave the gloomy passages there, because they did indeed describe a part of the real world that a person of Christ-following faith has to face. I wanted to say that real-world faith requires an unvarnished, totally objective view of the facts of evil and its consequences. Yet I hoped to challenge the reader with the idea that a Christ-follower can be, at the same time, an optimist because of God's promises of restoration and His call for us to be servants in the pursuit of that mission.

In that chapter I wanted to get the point across that even though we live with occasional suffering and loss, we can keep our heads up as Christ did. Bottom line? If you get blindsided by evil in any form, don't give in; don't lose heart; go on the offense and become even more bold. The power of the living Christ is more than adequate to overcome circumstances. That's the excitement within real-world faith.

I was in the middle of editing those remarks when the buzzer at the outside office door sounded. Standing there was a man in his thirties, neatly dressed, with great agitation on his face.

"You've got a problem, I hear," I said, hoping to put him at his ease.

"Yeah! My father told you?"

"I'm glad he called, and the timing was good because none of us are ordinarily here today. How much do you need?" I asked, taking my money out of my pocket. I had $42.00 which included two twenties I'd been carefully husbanding for the last two weeks in anticipation of an upcoming trip when I'd need a little extra in my pocket. I rarely carry much cash in New York, and so I breathed a prayer of thanksgiving that for some reason I had that much with me.

"I need $38.50. I'll bring you the receipt from the pharmacy right away. My father says he'll be here in an hour."

I couldn't think of why I'd need a receipt, but if he wanted to bring one back, that was OK with me.

Soon he was gone. I watched out the window as the man headed down Sixty-first Street and I remember wondering why he was walking in a direction where, as far as I knew, there were no pharmacies. But then I returned to my computer and the chapter on the sadness of life and the importance of never giving in to it.

Two hours passed, and I suddenly realized that I had not heard from the fellow to whom I'd given my two twenties—the one who was going to return with a receipt. Nor had I heard from the doctor—the one who said on the phone that he was grateful for my trust and would pay me back within the hour. *Perhaps the son had problems with his medication,* I thought, *and perhaps the doctor got caught in traffic on one of the bridges.* Those things happen in New York.

Another hour passed, and it was time to turn off the computer and head for the tram and our apartment. As I passed Dr. A——'s office, I saw the door open and a doorman standing there. On impulse I stopped and told him what had happened.

The man laughed. He laughed! "The doctor's been here all day and just left," he said. "He never would have called you for something like that. You've been taken. You got a quick course in Street Savvy."

I was instantly angry. I couldn't believe that someone could have sounded so convincing as he talked about neighborliness and trust. A minute later my anger turned toward myself. How could I have been so stupid? Why didn't I tell the man at the door that I'd walk with him to the pharmacy? Why hadn't I asked for some kind of identification? Then my anger became more generalized. I found myself thinking, *That's the last time I'll put out money on the spot for anyone who says he's in trouble.*

I headed home with a poisoned spirit. Suddenly, New York wasn't so beautiful anymore. The "lens" of affection through which I normally looked at the streets was clouded, and I found myself irritated at the garbage strewn on the curb, repelled by the beggar on the corner, annoyed at the ambulance siren, and irked by the fact that I'd missed the tram over to Roosevelt Island by ninety seconds. While I waited, I didn't want to talk to one of the maintenance men I knew, and when I got to our apartment building, I wasn't inclined to stop and visit with the doorman. All this because someone had cleverly conned me out of forty dollars.

When I told her what happened, Gail was as amused as the doorman at Dr. A——'s building. "I can't believe that someone as smart as you would not have thought to check him out," she said. That observation only compounded my unhappiness.

My imagination began to work. I grumped to Gail, "I bet the guy walked down the block with those two twenties and said to himself, 'That jerk would have given me every dime he had; I should have asked him for a hundred.'"

My imagination was of no value to my spirit, and I heard myself declare, "Well, all I've got to say is that's the last time I. . . ."

"No, it's not the last time you'll be generous," Gail interrupted, knowing where I was headed. "You can't write and talk about the sadness and unfairness of life and then become upset the minute your remarks prove to be true. We came to New York knowing that some of those people were around. We just thought they had less-sophisticated methods. So now we're a little wiser, but we're not going to be less compassionate."

Gail was right, but I gave myself a few more hours to sulk before I resolved the matter. The forgiveness I gave the inventive mugger came only late into the night, long after he was probably in his bed deep in sleep. Let him sleep; I was the one who had thinking to do.

I tried to bring meaning to what had happened by sorting out what bothered me so much. It really wasn't the forty dollars after all. And I could accept the embarrassment of seeming like such a naive victim in a con game. No, what really hurt was the fact that someone took advantage of my enthusiasm to be a kingdom servant. Someone, not knowing what he was doing, had shown contempt for my wonderful mission of expanding Christ's presence and power into dark situations.

Then with a burst of insight I got the message. If I was truly ready to follow Christ into the third dimension of the real world, I had to be prepared to take the same kind of bullets He'd taken. Jesus had entered a world full of con artists, and some of them played for much higher stakes than the one I met. Although the Lord saw each of them coming, He never wrote them off. He kept offering them grace until they crucified Him. I brooded on the fact that just before He died, one of the last people to whom He spoke generous words was a thief. And He invited him home . . . into the presence of His Father.

And then I remembered the words of Luther I had included in an earlier chapter: "He who will not suffer [to be in the midst of his enemies] does not want to be of the Kingdom of Christ; he wants to be among friends, to sit among the roses and lilies, not with the bad people but the devout people." Having said this, Luther had shouted out with his pen, *"If Christ had done what you are doing, who would have ever been spared?"* (emphasis mine).

I was rebuked! It was as if Christ was saying, "Let's you and Me take another walk into your inner space. I want you to tell Me what you think of some of the attitudes you've been nursing over this forty-dollar deal. What's this anger all about? These vengeful feelings? This sudden notion that every person with a need is crooked? Are you prepared to justify these things when you enter the Heavenlies in the morning and stand before the altar? If this is the level of your feelings when you lose a few dollars, what would your reaction be if you'd been shot or beaten to an pulp?"

I thought I heard Christ saying, "I want to test whether or not you believe what you've been trying to write in that book. I want to know if you can stand living in a real world where the good guys and the bad guys look just the same. I think it's time to find out whether grace is something you only want to receive but don't want to give."

I realized that every part of my real-world faith was being tested in this microcosmic moment of insight. How could one follow Christ into the presence of God and worship the Lamb slain for our sins if one came carrying a load of resentment? And how could one keep the doorway to the inner space open for Christ to enter if there was a lot of embarrassing inner "garbage" piled high and untended? And how could one really believe that he was called to make a little history in the streets as a servant of the Prince if he was instantly hostile the minute he got ripped off by people who were simply proving that, at times, life can be difficult and sad?

This book began with a picture of the smithy, that strong, hardworking man who stands at the forge and, despite the discomfort of the heat, makes the fire hotter. I wanted to visualize him pounding away at the molten metal, shaping it according to a particular purpose. I hoped that the picture would imprint itself upon our minds. And that we would see that every day is an opportunity to take our faith and beat it into further shape. I wanted us to see that faith is a proactive affair, and we must expand its influence within ourselves every day.

Faith is standing up in the heart and shouting, if necessary, "I believe in God the Father Almighty, the Maker, and I believe in Jesus

Christ, the crucified, risen, and ascended Lord, and I believe in the Holy Spirit, the Energizer of Christlike life!"

Faith is putting my life before Jesus and inviting His work of forgiveness for my sins and His challenge to carry the kingdom mandate into the world.

Faith is choosing to grow in Christlikeness and pushing myself to do it when others seem to be disinterested and to pursue self-serving objectives.

Faith is affirming that nothing I have (my body, my skills, my possessions, my money) is mine but belongs to the Lord God Creator. As He has been generous to me, so must I be generous in response both to Him and to others.

And faith is looking out upon a world that was never meant to be this way and grieving over it as Christ did. Not a grief that is patronizing or marked with an air of superiority. But a grief that identifies and accepts responsibility: "I and my fathers have sinned."

Finally, faith is hope. Hope that in every day, I can make a little history that will leave creation and humanity a tiny bit better than the day before. And hope that one day Jesus will come and complete the job.

When real-world faith is heated up to molten temperatures through worship, self-exposure, and resolve to be a kingdom servant, the world takes on an entirely new perspective. The littlest things, once ignored, come alive with significance. Big things, once intimidating, are reduced to true size. Little people become valuable; celebrities become mere human beings. Nature becomes magnificent, and one leaps to the day with a dream of planting the presence of Christ in one more corner of a darkened world, whether it be in a dry cleaners or on the floor of the stock exchange, a campus library or a child's nursery. One of my favorite twentieth-century Christ-followers, Samuel Logan Brengle of the Salvation Army, wrote of a day when he came to an experience of faith that totally reoriented his perspective on the world:

> I walked over Boston Commons before breakfast, weeping for joy and praising God. Oh, how I loved! In that hour I knew Jesus, and I loved Him till it seemed my heart would break with love. I was filled with love for all His creatures. I heard the little sparrows chattering; I loved them. I saw a little worm wriggling across my path; I stepped over it. I did not want to hurt any living thing. I

loved the dogs, I loved the horses, I loved the little urchins on the
street, I loved the strangers who hurried past me, I loved the
heathen—I loved the whole world. (From Emile Calliet's *Journey
into Light, Z*)

What Brengle experienced was not an abhorrence for the world
but an explosive affection for it. He suddenly saw the world through
the eyes of Jesus, and everything changed.

Not long ago a relatively new Christ-follower came to me and
handed me an envelope. In it were fifteen ten-dollar bills. "I have to
give this to you," he said. "I've been feeling badly about something I
did a couple of years back, and when I prayed, I felt a leading that this
was the only way to make the proper restitution. Use this money
somewhere; it will do someone some good."

I was curious as to what he meant and asked him if he'd like to talk
about what was behind this decision.

"Sure," he said. "I have this camera at home that fell off the back
of a truck."

I looked at him incredulously. "You have a camera that did what?"

"Didn't you ever hear that expression before?" he said, grinning.
"That's a New York term for something that's hot, stolen. I bought a
hot camera from a guy a couple of years ago, and this is the amount of
money I should have paid if I'd been honest."

I put the envelope in my desk drawer for a couple of weeks and
actually forgot about it. And then one day when I was walking on Second Avenue I met a woman Gail and I know who has a very difficult
time making financial ends meet. She was disconsolate over further
disappointments in her life that she could not control.

My first reaction was to give her a few encouraging words and go
on my way. And then after I'd left her, I remembered the envelope. I
turned around, called to her, and asked if she would walk back to my
office with me. There I found the envelope, handed it to her, and told
her the story about the camera that had fallen off the truck.

"Look inside," I told her. "Make sure you know how much is in
there and then enjoy it."

She counted and began to weep. She actually began to do a little
dance there on the street. "I'm rich! I'm rich!" she rejoiced. "Thank
you, oh, thank you very much."

I walked down Sixty-first Street with some very strange feelings in
my heart. I was really impressed that there are people who compute

wealth in terms of $150. And I was further impressed and thankful that one more time I'd been able to press a little kingdom into a person's life. Together, all three of us, we'd put something back on the truck.

God had played a little trick on evil in that transaction. Someone had stolen a camera and fenced it. My friend had contributed to the evil of the process by buying it at a financial advantage to himself. But there had come a new day when he accepted the invitation of Christ to follow and had entered the Heavenlies and met God. That led to a process of self-exposure in which he followed Christ into his inner world. Repentance resulted, and in the process of that lifestyle had come a desire to resolve a regrettable memory of the past. The money had been passed to me, and out there on the streets, it moved into the hands of one who thought she was suddenly rich. A little bit of kingdom history was made.

That is the pleasure of real-world faith: following Christ in several different directions at once. All of life explodes with significance. In the Heavenlies, you more than likely will be blessed; in the inner self, you will probably be astonished; in the streets, you could get stung (but Christ was stung too, and as He said, "A servant is not greater than his Lord"). On the other hand, there are those wonderful moments in the streets when you get to be a part of a process that puts something that "fell off the truck" back where it belongs.

MEMO TO: Daniel
FROM: A Christ-follower

RE: A few thoughts from one smithy to another
Many thanks, Daniel, for several decades of incredible kingdom living. Thanks for giving us a grand view of the living God and what difference it makes to have a sound theology.

And thanks, Daniel, for being candid enough to let us know that life for you was a terrific struggle: disciplines, prayer life, awareness that you too were by nature a sinful man. Had you not confessed it, we would have found it hard to conceive that you ever had a problem.

And thanks one more time for a remarkable example of work under the most difficult circumstances: the way you handled pressure, the way you spoke hard things when they needed to be said, the way you kept your personal life spotless, the way you didn't fight back when people set out to get you. Thanks for showing us how to be points of light in a dark age.

Real-world faith makes a lot more sense now, Daniel, because you showed us how it works. And you did it in times every bit as tough as those in which we live.

A lot of men and women in our time are following Christ into the three sectors of the real world. Perhaps the greatest of them, according to Heaven's criteria, will never be noted by more than a very few. Their names and faces will never make our religious magazines, and they will never be invited to give banquet addresses and receive awards of honor.

They will simply live quietly in cities and villages doing the tasks of mothers, managers, salesmen, dry cleaners, government workers, farmers, and nurses. Some will be engineers, programmers, and military officers. Some will be delighted to be nannies, newscasters, social workers, and teachers. An occasional bystander will wonder at their seeming lack of importance. But God will know that a piece of the kingdom is being built where they are because they are at an anvil and they are forging a real-world faith.

In the third century St. Cyprian wrote to a friend named Donatus,

This seems a cheerful world, Donatus, when I view it from this fair garden under the shadow of these vines. But if I climbed some great mountain and looked out over the wide lands, you know very well what I would see. Brigands on the high road, pirates on the seas, in the amphitheaters men murdered to please the applauding crowds, under all roofs misery and selfishness. It is really a bad world, Donatus, an incredibly bad world.

Yet in the midst of it, I have found a quiet and holy people. They have discovered a joy which is a thousand times better than any pleasure of this sinful life. They are despised and persecuted, but they care not. They have overcome the world. These people, Donatus, are the Christians. . . . and I am one of them. (From Edward England's *The Unfading Vision*)